Starting Radical Churches

STARTING RADICAL CHURCHES

Multiply House Churches Using Ten Proven Church Planting Bible Studies

Daniel B Lancaster

Lightkeeper Press
Nashville, Tennessee

Starting Radical Churches/ Daniel B Lancaster

ISBN 978-1-5218464-3-8

Dedicated to Living Waters Fellowship

Hamilton, Texas

CONTENTS

PREFACE

My prayer is this book will strengthen your walk with God. May you draw closer to Jesus every day and be filled with the Spirit. May you have a deep sense in your spirit that God loves you and will help you defeat any fear.

I have included several bonus gifts that I believe will be a blessing to you. The free *Making Disciples Bonus Pak* which includes three resources to help you pray powerful prayers:

- *100 Promises Audio Version*
- *40 Discipleship Quotes*
- *40 Powerful Prayers*

All are suitable for framing. To download your free *Making Disciples Bonus Pak*, CLICK HERE

I've also included an excerpt from my bestselling book *Powerful Prayers in the War Room*. God has blessed many through this book and I wanted to give you a chance to "try before you buy." To order *Powerful Prayers in the War Room*, CLICK HERE.

If you like the book, please leave a review. Your feedback will help other believers find this book easier and encourage me in my calling to write practical, powerful books to encourage, equip, and empower Christians throughout the world.

Every Blessing,

Daniel B Lancaster

Nashville, Tennessee — December 2015

INTRODUCTION

Welcome to *Starting Radical Churches*, part three of the Follow Jesus Training series (FJT)! May God bless and prosper you as you follow his Son. May your ministry grow exponentially as you walk slowly with Jesus through your unreached people group (UPG).

The manual you hold in your hands is a training workshop for planting biblical churches based on Jesus' strategy to reach the world. The result of years of research and testing in North America and Southeast Asia, these materials are not theory, but practice. Use these lessons and principles to bear much fruit as you join Jesus on his mission to the world.

Starting Radical Churches is practical training that equips believers to follow the fourth step of Jesus' strategy to reach the nations: start groups that lead to churches. We can trace Jesus' tactics through the Gospels, the book of Acts, the Epistles, and Church History. The goal of Follow Jesus Training is transformation, not information. As a result, lessons are simple "seeds" of key spiritual truths so believers can easily share them with others. Following the spiritual principle "A little leaven leavens the whole lump," they inspire believers to become reproducing, passionate followers of Christ.

After starting a rural church and a suburban church in America, our family sensed a call to Southeast Asia to coach and train leaders. I had been a church planter in America for ten years and coached other church planters, too. God had blessed our ministry in America and we were sure he would do the same overseas. Our family left for the mission field with hubris and high hopes.

During language learning, I began to train others with a national partner. We started by offering a one-week training course on basic discipleship and church planting. Typically, 30 to 40 students would come to the training. They often expressed appreciation and commented on how the lessons were helpful. Nevertheless, one issue began to concern me: it was obvious they were not teaching others what they had learned.

Teaching learners in a way they could teach the same lesson to others did not concern us in America. I think the main reason is a biblical understanding existed at the center of American culture in the Bible belt where we ministered, even among lost people. In Southeast Asia, however, no biblical understanding exists among the lost. On the mission field, you cannot assume a person will meet another Christian who will influence them.

We faced our first significant problem in mission work. We were teaching nationals what we felt was "good stuff," but they were not reproducing it. In fact, it seemed like we were attracting "Professional seminar goers." Providing meals at the weeklong training in a country overwhelmed with poverty mired the results, as well. What happened next surprised and humbled me.

After one of our training events, I sat down in a teashop with my interpreter and asked him a simple question:

"John. How much of the training we did this week do you think the folks will do and train others to do?"

John thought about it for a while and I could tell he did not want to answer me. In his culture, a student should never comment on his teacher's performance, and he felt like that was what I was asking him to do. After more conversation and assurances from me, he gave a response that changed everything:

"Dr. Dan, I think they will do about ten percent of what you taught them this past week."

Stunned, I tried not to show it. Instead, I asked John another question:

"John, can you show me the ten percent you think they will do or are doing? My plan is to keep that ten percent, discard the rest, and rewrite the training until they do everything we train them to do."

John showed me the ten percent he believed they would do. We culled the rest and rewrote the training for the next meeting. One month later, we offered another weeklong training, and I asked John the same question afterwards: What percent will they do?

John said, "Dr. Dan, I estimate they will do 15 percent of what you taught this time."

I was speechless. What John did not know is that I had rewritten the training from the previous month. I had inserted the "best of the best" of everything I had learned as an American pastor and church planter coach. I had created the best training seminar I could… and the learners were only going to give 15 percent of the lessons to others!

Thus began the method that we used for two and a half years, refining and developing the Follow Jesus Training system. Each month, we taught a one-week seminar and received comments after the seminar. One question guided our efforts: what percent of what we taught them will they do (or are doing) because of the training?

By the third month, our percentage rose to twenty percent. The next month, it went to twenty-five percent. Some months we made no progress at all. Other months, we leaped ahead. Throughout the development phase, a clear principle emerged; the more we trained learners to follow Jesus' example, the more likely they were to train others to do the same.

I still remember the day John and other nationals shared with me the people we had trained were doing 90 percent of what we had taught them to do. We had long since left our western methods, our Asian methods, our PhD training, our experiences, and learned instead to trust only in the example Jesus left us to follow. That is how we developed FJT in Southeast Asia.

As we continued to make disciples, they formed "Simple worship" groups. In these groups, they loved God with all of their heart by worshipping him. They loved God with all of their soul by praying to him. They loved God with all of their mind by studying his word. Finally, they loved God with all of their strength by practicing what they had learned. With confidence from practice, learners could spiritually minister to others. These groups multiplied and grew easily, even in countries hostile to the gospel.

A new issue began to surface in our work—a problem many

missionaries face today. The issue centered on defining in our cultural context "What is a true church?" Several discipleship groups wanted to become a church, but were unsure how to form a church. Some discipleship groups claimed to be churches, but never shared baptism or the Lord's Supper. Other groups had already become churches, but still considered themselves a discipleship group. Still other long-standing "churches" were nothing more than discipleship groups. Adding to the confusion were denominational definitions of a church that insisted on 50 baptized members, a building, and a full-time pastor.

What troubled us the most about this issue was the "identity crisis" the confusion caused among discipleship groups and churches we coached. Both groups walked with a halting step, unsure of their standing before God and man. Instead of the peace that Jesus promised, tension and misunderstanding spread among the discipleship groups and churches.

The solution to these problems eluded us for some time, until we went back to the bedrock of everything God had shown us about following Jesus' example. Insights from George Patterson about the Great Commission and teaching others to obey Jesus' commands provided an important turning point. Patterson had shown that the Apostles taught the first church to obey seven of Jesus' commands. A group that committed to follow the seven commands of Christ qualified as a church. Size of group, a building, or a full-time pastor were not the determinants, but Jesus' commands. This simple definition removed cultural, historical, and denominational baggage and allowed us to coach nationals to start churches unique to their culture.

After a thorough study of the first four chapters of the book of Acts, we eventually developed a list of nine commands of Jesus the Early Church obeyed. *Starting Radical Churches* contains ten lessons based on those commands and a healthy group decision-making process. Use this material to help a discipleship group that wants to become a church make that transition. The mission field is ripe with discipleship groups that could become churches if they had simple coaching and a proven method. You have the ability to give them both with *Starting Radical Churches* training.

> It is with cheerfulness that we dismiss our twelves, our twenties, our fifties to form other churches. We encourage our members to leave us to found other churches; nay, we seek to persuade them to do it. We ask them to scatter throughout the land, to become the goodly seed, which God shall bless. I believe that so long as we do this, we shall prosper. I have marked other churches that have adopted the other way, and they have not succeeded.
> —Charles Spurgeon

PART I

NUTS & BOLTS

FOLLOW JESUS TRAINING

When the realization of his controlling method finally dawns on the open mind of the disciple, he will be amazed at its simplicity and wonder how he could have ever failed to see it before. Nevertheless, when his plan is reflected on, the basic philosophy is so different from that of the modern church that its implications are nothing less than revolutionary.
—Robert C. Coleman

Jesus' strategy to reach the nations includes five tactics: grow strong in God, share the gospel, make disciples, start groups that lead to churches, and train leaders. Each stands alone, but they build on one another to create a fruitful ministry. The material in Follow Jesus Training enables trainers to be a spark for a multiplication movement among their people, simply by following Jesus.

Making Radical Disciples

Follow Jesus Training begins with *Making Radical Disciples*, which covers the first three tactics in Jesus' strategy. Disciples learn how to pray, obey Jesus' commands, and walk in the power of the Holy Spirit (Be Strong in God). Disciples then discover how to join God where he is working and share their testimony—a powerful weapon in spiritual warfare. Next, they learn how to share the gospel and invite people back to God's family (Share the Gospel).

Completing the course provides leaders with the tools to start a small group, cast a vision for multiplication, and a plan to reach their community (Start Groups).

Growing disciples expressed two felt needs as we trained and coached them. Emerging leaders often asked how to grow as spiritual leaders. They wondered what steps were necessary to transition from a group to a church. Because the tactics in Jesus' strategy are not sequential, some disciples asked for leadership training and then church planting training. Other disciples reversed that order. As a result, we began to offer two extra training seminars to disciples who used *Making Radical Disciples* and were faithful to train others.

Training Radical Leaders

Training Radical Leaders helps leaders develop others to become passionate, spiritual leaders—the fifth tactic in Jesus' strategy. A key ingredient in multiplication movements is leadership development. The seminar shows leaders the process Jesus used to train leaders and the seven leadership qualities of Jesus, the greatest leader of all-time.

Leaders discover their personality type and ways to help people with different personalities work together. Finally, leaders develop a "Jesus Plan" based on 12 ministry principles Jesus gave the disciples in Luke 10. The seminar closes with leaders sharing their "Jesus Plan" and praying with one another. Leaders commit to coaching one another and developing new leaders in the future.

Starting Radical Churches

Starting Radical Churches aids a disciple group in moving from being a disciple group to becoming a church—the fourth tactic in Jesus' strategy. Few leaders have started a church, and one frequent mistake planters make is copying their current church in the new church plant.

This approach almost guarantees meager results for several reasons. Every church, like every person, has a unique personality and copying what worked at one church does not guarantee success at another. Copying another church also blinds church leaders from seeking a church that meets the needs of their community. Finally, small churches that "act" like a larger church (the mother church) do not survive long because the weight of the mother church's structure is too much to bear.

Starting Radical Churches avoids this mistake by training disciples how to follow the nine commands of Christ the disciples taught the Early Church in Acts 2. The group works through practical applications of each command and develops a church covenant together. If the group senses God's leading, the seminar ends with a ceremony of celebration and dedication as a new church.

Both *Starting Radical Churches* and *Training Radical Leaders* train disciples how to copy Jesus' ministry and method. Trainers give leaders reproducible tools they can master and share with others. *Follow Jesus Training* is not a course to learn, but a way to live. For more than two thousand years, God has blessed and changed countless lives through the simplicity of following his Son. Believers have followed Jesus' strategy and seen whole cultures transformed. May God do the same in your life and among the people group you train to follow Jesus.

STARTING RADICAL CHURCHES

You would be wrong to think that church planting movements are a white man's idea. They are not. We are trying to implement in the west what we are seeing God do all over the developing world. We have been the last to get it.
—Bob Roberts Jr.

Training Results

Starting Radical Churches builds on the first course, *Making Radical Disciples*, and helps those who have started disciple group's transition those groups into healthy house churches. After completing this training seminar, learners can:

- Teach leaders how to transition a disciple group to a house church using ten core church-planting lessons
- Train church members using a reproducible method modeled by Jesus
- Lead a group planning and problem-solving process with their new church
- Understand and carry out the Great Confession, Great Commandment, and Great Commission among their people group

Training Principles

We discovered the following principles amid training thousands of believers the last 11 years. In our experience, the principles are not culturally specific; we have seen them work around the world.

Less Is Better than More — most Christians know more of the Bible than they obey. A common mistake among trainers is giving their learners far more information than they can obey. Long-term exposure to training like this leaves learners full of knowledge with little practical application. We always try to give the learner a "backpack" of information they can carry with them and apply, not a "crate."

Different Learners Learn in Different Ways — people approach learning from three different styles: auditory, visual, and kinesthetic. For training to be reproducible, learners should experience all three styles of learning during a session. Western training events, however, usually rely on one or two styles and ignore the rest. Our goal is to see transformation across an entire group of people. Our training system, as a result, incorporates all three learning styles to exclude no one.

Both Process and Content Are Important — researchers have discovered many advances in adult education that teach people in a transformational, rather than informational, way. For example, research has shown the lecture format is not a good method for most students. Unfortunately, teachers use this format most often. Sadly, most training done overseas still follows this pattern. We concentrate on reproducibility in the

Follow Jesus Training system—evaluating our lessons on the ability of the next generation of learners to reproduce them.

Review, Review, Review — a phrase often used for memorizing is "Learning something by heart." Our training system is all about seeing people's hearts transformed. A goal in Follow Jesus Training is for every student to recite the entire training course from memory at the end of the course. The "Review" sections in each session and hand motions help learners to do just that. Please do not skip the review. In our experience, even third-grade educated rice farmers in Southeast Asia can recite the entire contents of this material because of repetition and the use of hand motions.

Build the Lesson — when we train others, we "build" the lesson to aid memorization and increase the confidence of the learners. For example, we ask the first question, read the scripture, give the answer, and show the hand motion. Then, we read the second question and follow the same process. Before we continue to the third question, however, we review the question, answer, and hand motion for questions one and two. Then, we go to question three. We follow this same pattern throughout the lesson, "building up" the lesson with each new question. This helps learners to understand the whole lesson in context and remember it better. All the lessons in this study include a review part. Repetition plants God's truth deep in our hearts and brings a fruitful harvest.

Be an Example — people do what they see modeled for them. Genuine training means living out the material ourselves and not merely teaching information to others. Fresh stories about how

God is working in our own lives inspire those we train. Training believers to follow Jesus is not a job, but a lifestyle. Multiplication movements occur in direct relationship to the number of believers in a people group who have adopted this attitude

Training Method

Sessions in *Starting Radical Churches* follow the same format: worship, prayer, study, practice, and the grow process. A basic lesson outline follows with suggested times:

Worship

- The group sings two choruses or hymns together
- Five minutes

Prayer

- Partners share prayer concerns and pray for each other
- Ten minutes

Study

- The trainer teaches a reproducible church planting lesson that gives insight and skills needed to become a healthy church
- Twenty minutes

Practice

- Learners divide into groups of four and practice

teaching one another the church planting lesson
- Twenty minutes

GROW

Learners discuss the best way to carry out what they have learned in their group.

"G" Stands For "Goal"

- The leader presents the church planting goal of the session
- Five minutes

"R" Stands For "Roadblocks"

- The group talks about different roadblocks they face in obeying this command of Jesus in their group
- Ten minutes

"O" Stands For "Options"

- The leader asks group members to come up with a list of at least ten ways they can overcome the Roadblocks
- Ten minutes

"W" Stands For "What Does God Want?"

- The group write their commitment to obey this command in the church covenant
- Ten minutes

SAMPLE
CHURCH
COVENANT

As members of God's family known as
_____ church, we covenant before God
and one another to:

> Declare the Great Confession that Jesus is the Christ, the
> Son of the living God. Matthew 16:15–18

> Follow the Great Commandment to love God with all of
> our heart, soul, mind, and strength; and to love our neigh-
> bor as ourselves. Mark 12:30–31

> Obey the Great Commission to go into the entire world,
> making disciples, baptizing them in the name of the
> Father, the Son, and the Holy Spirit. We will teach them
> to obey everything Jesus has commanded. Matthew
> 28:18–20

As a covenant body of believers, present and future, we affirm
that Jesus is with us until the end of the age. We commit to
following the same basic commands of Christ the Apostles
taught the early churches to obey.

> *Repent* — we turn away from our sin to the living God,
> choosing to walk his path and not our own. Mark 1:15

Believe — we put our trust and faith in Jesus Christ and believe he is the way, the truth, and the life. John 14:1

Baptize — we have followed the Lord in baptism and will help new believers to do the same. Matthew 28:19

Make Disciples — we choose to live richly in the word of God and teach others how to obey Jesus' commands in their everyday lives. Matthew 28:20

Love — we strive to love one another the same way that Christ loves us. John 15:17

Remember — we commit to celebrating the Lord's Supper together as a body. Matthew 26:26–28

Pray — we commit to pray for church members and the world. We will continually ask for God's kingdom to come and his will be done on earth as it is in heaven. Matthew 6:9

Give — each believer in our church will give as the Lord directs with a cheerful heart. By God's grace, we will meet the needs of our church, our city, and the world. Luke 6:38

Worship — we commit to meet weekly as a body of believers to dwell richly in the word of God, encouraging one another, singing psalms, hymns, and spiritual songs with thanksgiving in our hearts. John 4:24

Signed   this   _____   day   of   the   month
_____ in the year _____.

Signatures:

F.A.Q.

What does a multiplication movement look like?

David Garrison, in *Church Planting Movements*, lists ten universal elements of a multiplication movement:

- Vitality of prayer in the missionary's personal life that leads to its imitation in the life of the new church and its leaders
- Abundant gospel sowing, often relying heavily upon mass media evangelism, but also including personal evangelism with vivid testimonies to the life-changing power of the gospel
- Someone implements a strategy of deliberate church planting
- Even among non-literate people groups, the Bible is the guiding source for doctrine, church polity and life itself
- Missionaries coach nationals how to start churches, rather than starting new churches themselves
- Reliance upon bi-vocational lay leaders who match the general profile of the people group where they minister
- The vast majority of churches average 20 members and meet in homes or store fronts
- Usually, missionaries plant the first churches, but

national believers start subsequent churches following an easily reproduced model
- Churches are unencumbered by nonessential elements and the laity are fully empowered to partici-
pate in what God is doing, leading to rapid growth of
disciples, groups, and churches
- Churches practice the five purposes of a healthy
church (worship, evangelism, discipleship, ministry,
and fellowship)

What are the differences between disciple groups and churches?

Some believers struggle to know the difference between a discipleship group and church because there are many similarities,
especially if they attend a house church.

In our experience, we have seen disciple groups who were
really churches and groups that thought they were a church,
but were actually a disciple group. Confusion abounds.

Typically, the differences between a disciple group and a
church are three: observing the Lord's Supper, baptizing
believers, and taking an offering.

Jesus never set a certain number of people needed to be an "Offi-
cial" church. He also did not say a group must have a building or
full-time minister. He did give commands the disciples taught the
early churches to follow, however. We teach discipleship groups
to obey the bedrock commands and covenant to become a church.

What should I do if my denomination only allows ordained ministers to baptize believers or lead the Lord's Supper, but none are available?

Our goal as followers of Christ is to love and live at peace, showing the love of Jesus. If there is an organized group of Christians who believe in Jesus, follow his word, and have the same goals as your group, we encourage you to form partnerships with them in the ministry.

Denominations usually have clauses in their bylaws for circumstances when ministers who baptize and perform the Lord's Supper are not available. Typically, denominations encourage outside pastors to delegate their authority to trusted workers in the local church. We encourage you to contact respected pastors and ask them to lay hands on you and set you aside to do the baptism or serve the Lord's Supper.

We have seen several settings, however, where a denomination or local pastors were unwilling to cooperate with earnest workers. Whether because of jealousy or a need to control, leaders commanded lay leaders not to baptize or observe the Lord's Supper. In a case like this, we encourage you to follow the example of Peter and John in Acts 5:29. They answered the council saying, "We must obey God, rather than men."

What is the "Rule of Five?"

Learners must practice a lesson five times before they have the confidence necessary to train another person.

The first time, the learners say, "That was such a good lesson. Thank you for teaching us."

The second time (after they have taught the lesson), they will say, "I think maybe I can teach this lesson, but I am not sure."

The third time, the learners say, "This lesson is not as hard to teach as I thought. Maybe I can train my friends to teach this lesson after all."

The fourth time, learners say, "I can see how important this lesson is and I want to teach others. It is getting easier each time."

The fifth time, learners say, "I can train others to train others how to do this lesson. I am confident God will use this lesson to change the lives of my friends and family."

Someone follows the "Rule of Five" when that person actively takes part or teaches a lesson five times. For that reason, we recommend doing the practice time twice. Each time the learners repeat teaching the lesson, it plants itself deeper into their hearts.

Why do you use hand motions?

The hand motions may seem childish at first, but people soon realize the physical activity helps them to memorize the material more quickly. Using hand motions aids those with kinesthetic and visual learning styles.

Be careful using the hand motions, however! Check the local customs of those you are training and make sure none of the hand motions are in poor taste or mean something different from you intend. We field-tested the hand motions in this manual in several Southeast Asia countries, but checking ahead of time is still a good idea.

Don't be surprised if doctors, lawyers, and other more-educated learners enjoy learning and doing the hand motions. A comment we hear often is "Finally! Here are lessons I can teach others and they will understand and do them."

Why are the lessons so simple?

Jesus trained in a simple, memorable way. We use real-life examples (skits) and stories because that is what Jesus did. We believe a lesson is reproducible only if it can pass the napkin test. Can learners write the lesson on a paper napkin over a casual meal? Can he or she teach a partner the lesson immediately?

The lessons in *Starting Radical Churches* "teach themselves" and depend on the Holy Spirit to plant good seed. Simplicity is the key factor in reproducibility.

We recommend teaching the material in this manual as it is, without changing anything at least five times (other than adapting the training to the cultural setting where you work). Imagine our training team walking beside you, guiding you the first five times you hold this training. *Starting Radical Churches* has several underlying forces that are not obvious until you have trained others step-by-step several times.

So far, we have trained thousands of believers with reproducible lessons throughout Asia and America. Follow this suggestion to avoid mistakes others have already made! Remember: a smart man learns from his mistakes; a wise man learns from the mistakes of others

What are some common mistakes people make when they train others?

Skipping The Accountability Part of the Training — worship, prayer, and Bible study compose the typical small group meeting. Training includes these three, but adds accountability with a practice time. Most people do not believe they can hold others accountable and keep the friendship, so they skip this part. By setting an example and asking nonjudgmental questions, however, a group can hold one another accountable and see significant spiritual growth.

Focusing on One Person and Not a Group — the idea of one-on-one discipleship is good in theory, but falls short in practice. The biblical norm is making disciples in a small-group setting. Jesus spent the most time with Peter, James, and John. A group of men accompanied Peter on his church-planting journeys and helped in the church at Jerusalem. Lists of the groups of people Paul discipled fill his letters.

Expecting Too Much Too Soon — realize only about 10 to 15 percent of the people you train will train others. Don't let this fact discourage you. Even with this percentage, God will bring about a multiplication movement if we are faithful to cast the gospel seed broadly.

Talking Too Much — in a typical 90-minute session, the trainer speaks to the group 30 minutes. Learners spend most of the time in a training session in joint worship, prayer, sharing, and practice. Many from a western educational background fall into the trap of reversing this time order.

Training in a Non-Reproducible Way — disciples who can reproduce themselves are the key to a multiplication movement.

The most important people you are training, then, are not current attendees. The critical people are the third and fourth generations of disciples training other disciples.

Forget the Purpose of Training — settling into old teaching patterns is easy. A guiding question to keep the training on track is "Will disciples in following generations be able to copy what I am teaching and pass it to others? Will the fourth generation of believers be able to share these lessons in their training sessions? Would they be successful?" If they can follow you easily, it is reproducible. Lessons that do not connect with their culture and education level are not reproducible.

What should I do if there are no churches willing to start other churches?

Churches do not start other churches for various reasons. Coaching leaders with the grow process will help them identify the roadblocks to obeying Jesus' commands their congregation faces.

For some churches, the problems center on knowledge. They do not know that Jesus commanded the church to go into the world and that means starting new churches. Others do not know anyone interested in starting churches. The purpose of this manual is to fill the knowledge gaps that block churches from obeying Jesus.

Other churches struggle with vision. A lack of vision produces a lack of motivation. A lack of prayer and not enough faith cause churches to have small visions. As you pray and cast vision, others will begin to see what God is doing in the world and want to join him.

The most common reason churches do not start churches, however, is they do not know how. This manual gives a simple method of how to help discipleship groups become house churches—a process that involves obeying nine basic commands of Christ. Leaders also learn a problem-solving method they can use in the future anytime they face obstacles in their ministry.

How should I prepare for a training seminar?

Enlist a Prayer Team — recruit a prayer team of 12 people to intercede for the training, before and during the training week. Prayer is important!

Enlist an Apprentice — recruit an apprentice to team-teach with you, someone who has previously attended *Starting Radical Churches*.

Invite Participants — encourage participants to come in a culturally sensitive way. Send letters, invitations, or make telephone calls. If you are training people from different groups, the best size group for a *Starting Radical Churches* training is 16 to 24 learners. If you are helping an established disciple group transition to a church, size of group does not matter.

Confirm Logistics — arrange housing, meals, and transport for leaders as needed.

Secure a Meeting Place — in a training seminar setting, arrange a meeting room with two tables for supplies in the back of the room. Set up participant chairs in a circle and allow plenty of room for learning activities during the sessions. In some cultures, provide mats on the floor instead of chairs. Plan to provide two break times every day with coffee, tea, and snacks.

Gather Training Materials — collect Bibles, a white board or large sheets of paper, student notes, leader notes, color markers or crayons. Provide notebooks like the ones students use in school, pens or pencils, and the Church Covenant Worksheet.

Arrange Worship Times — use song sheets or a chorus book for each participant. Find a person in the group who plays guitar and ask him or her to help you lead the worship times.

What should I do after we complete the training seminar?

Evaluate Every Part of the Training with Your Apprentice — spend time reviewing and evaluating the training time with your apprentice. Create a list of positives and negatives. Make plans to improve the training next time you teach it.

Connect with Possible Apprentices — contact people who showed budding leadership ability during the training sessions. Ask them to help you with a *Starting Radical Churches* training in the future.

Encourage Participants to Bring Friends to the Next Training — urge participants to return with ministry partners the next time they attend. Doing so will speed up the number of leaders who train other leaders to transition discipleship groups to churches.

PART II

LESSONS

1

A GREAT
CHURCH

See the gospel church secure, and founded on a rock! All her promises are sure;
her bulwarks who can shock? Count her every precious shrine; tell, to after-ages
tell, fortified by power divine, the church can never fail.
—Charles Wesley

Learners can expect the following results in this lesson:

- Understand the foundation of a great church
- Repeat from memory the nine basic commands of Jesus that form a church
- Memorize Acts 9:31
- Practice training one another using the "A Great Church" lesson
- Discuss how much it costs to start a church and how Jesus views new churches

Worship

Sing two choruses or hymns together.

Prayer

Ask a respected leader to pray for God's presence and blessing during the training seminar.

Study

What is a church?

Ask learners to turn to a blank page in their notebook.

"We are going to have a drawing contest with prizes. First place will get the biggest prize, second place a smaller prize, and third place will be even smaller."

Tell learners they have 3 minutes to draw the best picture of a church they can. After 3 minutes, ask learners to stop drawing and begin judging the contest.

[Judging the contest] Walk around the group while they are drawing their pictures. Most people will draw a picture similar to the church they attend. Contest winners should draw more than a church building, but show people, a flock, a body, etc. Announce winners and explain why they won as a transition into the lesson.

What confession does Jesus say his followers believe?

Let's read Matthew 16:15–18 aloud together.

> *"But what about you?" He asked. "Who do*
> *you say I am?"*
>
> *Simon Peter answered, "You are the Messiah,*
> *the Son of the living God."*
>
> *Jesus replied, "Blessed are you, Simon Son of Jonah, for this was*
> *not revealed to you by flesh and blood, but by my Father in*
> *heaven. And I tell you that you are Peter, and on this rock I will*
> *build my church, and the gates of Hades will not overcome it.*
> *Matthew 16:15–18*

Jesus establishes a church's foundation the confession that he is the Christ, the Son of the living God. Jesus builds his church with those who have confessed faith in him. He promises the gates of hell cannot prevail against his church.

A church must believe Jesus is the Savior who entered our world to save men from their sins. Jesus is the Christ. A church must also believe that Jesus is the Son of God—fully God and fully man.

Most believers call Peter's confession the Great Confession, and we will do the same. Let's draw a circle and label it Great Confession to show the foundation of a church.

On a whiteboard, draw a circle and label it Great Confession.

Let's Review...

What confession does Jesus say his followers believe?

What commandment does Jesus say his followers obey?

Let's read Mark 12:30–31 aloud together.

> "Love the Lord your God with all your heart and with all your
> soul and with all your mind and with all your strength. The
> second is this: 'Love your neighbor as yourself.' There is no
> commandment greater than these." Mark 12:30–31

The two most important commands a church should follow
are love God and love people.

Most believers call these commands the Great Commandment and we will do the same.

Draw another circle with me and label it Great Commandment to show how Jesus builds his church.

Let's Review...

What confession does Jesus say his followers believe?

What commandment does Jesus say his followers obey?

Let's read Matthew 28:18–20 aloud together.

> Then Jesus came to them and said, "All authority in heaven and
> on earth has been given to me. Therefore go and make disciples
> of all nations, baptizing them in the name of the Father and of
> the Son and of the Holy Spirit, and teaching them to obey
> everything I have commanded you. And surely I am with
> you always, to the very end of the age." Matthew 28:18–20

Jesus commissioned his followers to make disciples. He told his followers to baptize the new disciples in the name of the Father, Son, and Holy Spirit. He also commanded them to teach the new disciples to obey all his commands. Most believers call this statement the Great Commission, and we will follow their example in these lessons.

Draw the final circle and label it Great Commission.

The church's foundation is faith that Jesus is Savior of the world and the Son of God: the Great Confession. Then, the church grows by loving God with all their heart, soul, mind, and strength; and loving people: the Great Commandment. Finally, Jesus commanded the church to make disciples, baptize them, and teach them to obey his commands: the Great Commission.

We draw the circles like this because the Great Confession, Great Commandment, and Great Commission are equally important. They influence and affect one another. Like a three-legged stool, each depends on the other to stand strong. Remove a leg from the stool and the stool falls. Remove one 'Great' from the church and the church will fail.

Let's Review...

What confession does Jesus say his followers believe?

What commandment does Jesus say his followers obey?

What commission does Jesus say his followers carry out?

What commands of Jesus did the Apostles teach the early church first?

Jesus commanded us in the Great Commission to teach people to obey his commands. We understand the core of a church by learning the nine commands of Christ the disciples taught the Early Church first.

> Repent – put one hand on top of another and push them down to your side. Turn your head like you are turning away from sin.

Let's practice this hand motion together. The first command is to repent. Let's do the hand motion three times together.

> Believe – Cross your hands over your heart and then lift your hands in worship.

The second command is to believe. Let's practice the hand motion three times together.

So, the first command is to repent (do the hand motion) and the second command is to believe (do the hand motion).

> Baptize – Hold elbow of right arm with left hand. Move right arm down to the right side, and then move back up to the starting position, mirroring the motion of baptism.

The third command is to baptize. Let's practice the hand motion three times together.

Let's Review.

The first command is to repent (do the hand motion). The sec-

STARTING RADICAL CHURCHES   39

ond is to believe (do the hand motion). The third is to baptize (do the hand motion).

> *Make Disciples — Hold hands together as if you are reading a book. Move "The book" forward and backward from the left side to the right side as if you are training others to follow Jesus.*

The fourth command is to make disciples. Let's practice the hand motion three times together.

Let's Review.

The first command is to repent (do the hand motion). The second is to believe (do the hand motion). The third is to baptize (do the hand motion). The fourth is to make disciples (do the hand motion).

> *Love — Clasp hands together as if you are shaking hands. Then, make a heart shape with both hands.*

The fifth command is to love. Let's practice the hand motion three times together.

Let's Review.

The first command is to repent (do the hand motion). The second is to believe (do the hand motion). The third is to baptize (do the hand motion). The fourth is to make disciples (do the hand motion). The fifth is to love (do the hand motion).

> *Remember — Put middle finger in the palm of the other hand and repeat with the other hand (sign language for crucifixion)*

The sixth command is to remember. Let's practice the hand motion three times together.

Let's Review.

The first command is to repent (do the hand motion). The second is to believe (do the hand motion). The third is to baptize (do the hand motion). The fourth is to make disciples (do the hand motion). The fifth is to love (do the hand motion). The sixth is to remember with the Lord's Supper (do the hand motion).

> *Pray – Form the classic "Praying hands" picture with your hands.*

The seventh command is to pray. Let's practice the hand motion three times together.

Let's Review.

The first command is to repent (do the hand motion). The second is to believe (do the hand motion). The third is to baptize (do the hand motion). The fourth is to make disciples (do the hand motion). The fifth is to love (do the hand motion). The sixth is to remember with the Lord's Supper (do the hand motion). The seventh is to pray (do the hand motion).

> *Give – Place both hands at chest level and then motion outwards as if you are giving something to someone.*

The eighth command is to give. Let's practice the hand motion three times together.

Let's Review.

The first command is to repent (do the hand motion). The second is to believe (do the hand motion). The third is to baptize (do the hand motion). The fourth is to make disciples (do the hand motion). The fifth is to love (do the hand motion). The sixth is to remember with the Lord's Supper (do the hand motion). The seventh is to pray (do the hand motion). The eighth is to give (do the hand motion).

Worship – Lift your hands in worship.

The ninth command is to worship. Let's practice the hand motion three times together.

Let's Review.

The first command is to repent (do the hand motion). The second is to believe (do the hand motion). The third is to baptize (do the hand motion). The fourth is to make disciples (do the hand motion). The fifth is to love (do the hand motion). The sixth is to remember with the Lord's Supper (do the hand motion). The seventh is to pray (do the hand motion). The eighth is to give (do the hand motion). And finally, the ninth is to worship (do the hand motion).

The first disciples taught the first church to obey these nine commands of Jesus. When a group of believers commits to obey these nine commands, they are a church.

Let's Review...

What confession does Jesus say his followers believe?

What commandment does Jesus say his followers obey?

What commission does Jesus say his followers carry out?

What commands of Jesus did the Apostles teach the Early Church first?

What is the memory verse?

Let's read Acts 9:31 aloud together.

> *Then the church throughout Judea, Galilee and Samaria*
> *enjoyed a time of peace and was strengthened. Living in the*
> *fear of the Lord and encouraged by the Holy Spirit, it increased*
> *in numbers. Acts 9:31*

Everyone stands and says the memory verse ten times together. The first six times, they use their Bible or lesson notes. The last four times, they say the verse from memory. Learners say the verse reference before quoting the verse each time and sit down when finished. Following this routine will help the trainers know what team has finished the lesson in the practice section.

Let's Review...

What confession does Jesus say his followers believe?

What commandment does Jesus say his followers obey?

What commission does Jesus say his followers carry out?

What commands of Jesus did the Apostles teach the Early Church first?

What is the memory verse?

Practice

Ask learners to divide into groups of four. If the large group has an odd number of people, one small group will have three members instead of four.

"Now we will practice the lesson to gain confidence so we can share it with friends and family. Jesus said to love God with all of your strength and practicing the lesson helps us do that. Teach the lesson to one another the same way we taught it to you. When you add a new question, practice repeating all the previous questions and answers, just as we did with you."

The first learner reads the first question, and the group reads the scripture aloud. Then, the first learner answers the question and helps the group learn the hand motion.

The second learner then reads the second question, the group reads the scripture aloud, and the second learner answers the question, helping the group learn the hand motion. Then, the second person asks the first question in review, and the group gives the answer with the hand motion. Next, the second learner asks the second question, and the group gives the answer with the hand motion.

Repeat this method going around the small group circle, each time adding a question, Scripture reading, answer, and hand motion until the group can repeat the entire lesson together.

Finally, follow the directions for saying the memory verse together.

GROW

How Much Does a New Church Cost?

Write a list of the nine commands of Christ on a whiteboard.

Go down the list of commands on the whiteboard, asking learners the cost to do each item. For example, how much money does it cost to repent? How much does believing cost? Write the answer beside the command.

"We think that churches need many materials: microphones, a keyboard, chairs, a building, etc. A church is a group of believers who commit to follow Jesus' commands together. And Jesus' commands do not cost any money. In reality, starting a church does not cost any money at all.

Let me ask again. How much does a new church cost? It does not take any money, just believers committing to follow Jesus' commands. In fact, research in America shows the more money spent starting a new church, the more likely the church will fail. Why do you think this is the case?"

Jesus Loves Baby Churches

Carry a pretend baby in your arms. Go around the group and "Show off your baby." Make a big deal about how beautiful your baby is.

Go to one of learners, show your baby, and share with the

group they said that your baby has ears like an elephant. Act offended, backing away from the learner.

Go to another learner, show your baby, and tell the group they said your baby has a nose like a pig. Act offended. Shield your baby from the learner.

Go to another learner, show your baby, and share with the group they said your baby has a tail like a monkey. Act as if you are angry. Ask learners, "What would you do if someone made these comments about your new baby?"

Explain that a group who decides to follow Jesus' basic commands, like the churches in the book of Acts, is a baby church. A new church may be small, but Jesus builds his church. Jesus passionately loves his church and does not like anyone criticizing his church as too small or not good enough.

2

REPENT

Some people do not like to hear much of repentance; but I think it is so necessary that if I should die in the pulpit, I would desire to die preaching repentance, and if out of the pulpit, I would desire to die practicing it.
—Matthew Henry

Learners can expect the following results in this lesson:

- Discuss the connection between Jesus, the Sunrise from on high, and the church as the light of the world
- Understand how to obey Jesus' command to repent
- Memorize Mark 1:15
- Practice training one another using the "Repent" lesson
- Use the grow process as a group to decide how to obey Jesus' command to repent

Worship

Sing two choruses or hymns together.

Prayer

Ask the group to divide into pairs.

Share prayer concerns you have and pray for each other. Also, pray for our study time that God would lead and direct us according to his will.

Study

Who is Jesus?

Let's read Luke 1:78–79 aloud together.

> *"Because of the tender mercy of our God, with which the Sunrise from on high will visit us, to shine upon those who sit in darkness and the shadow of death, to guide our feet into the way of peace." Luke 1:78–79 (NASB)*

Zechariah, the father of John the Baptist, prophesied about Jesus; he would be the "Sunrise from on high". Jesus is like the sun. He shines on those sitting in darkness: under the shadow of death. Jesus, the Sunrise, will guide our feet into the way of peace.

Let's Review...

Who is Jesus?

What is the church like?

Let's read Matthew 5:14–16 aloud together.

> You are the light of the world. A city set on a hill cannot be hidden; nor does anyone light a lamp and put it under a basket, but on the lamp stand, and it gives light to all who are in the house. Let your light shine before men in such a way that they may see your good works, and glorify your Father who is in heaven. Matthew 5:14–16 (NASB)

Jesus says the church is the light of the world. She is a city set on a hill that people can see far away. In the same way, people who light a lamp do not hide its light, but let it shine.

Jesus is the Sunrise and the Church is the Light

We obey Jesus' command to repent — to walk in the light

Jesus is the Sun and his church is the light. Jesus commands his church to let her light shine

Jesus is the Sunrise and the Church is the Light. We obey Jesus' command to repent — to walk in the light.

before men, so they will see the good the church does and glorify God.

Why is this important?

Take 5 minutes and discuss what it means for Jesus to be the Sunrise and the church the light of the world.

- Jesus is the source of our righteousness, we do good works because he lives in us.
- Jesus is the true light that has come into the world,

we shine to point others to him.
- Jesus is light and has no darkness, we seek to live a life of righteousness and truth to mirror him.

Let's Review...

Who is Jesus?

What is the church?

What did Jesus command the disciples?

Let's read Mark 1:15 aloud together.

> *"The time is fulfilled, and the kingdom of God has come near. Repent and believe in the good news!" Mark 1:15 (HCSB)*

Jesus told them the kingdom of God was close. He commanded them to repent and believe in the good news.

> *Repent – Put one hand on top of another and push them down to your side. Turn your head like you are turning away from sin.*

Let's Review...

Who is Jesus?

What is the church?

What did Jesus command the disciples?

How did the first churches obey?

Let's read Acts 2:38 aloud together.

> *Peter replied, "Repent and be baptized, every one of you, in the
> name of Jesus Christ for the forgiveness of your sins. And you
> will receive the gift of the Holy Spirit." Acts 2:38*

Peter told them to repent and be baptized in the name of Jesus
Christ. Jesus commanded people to repent and this is the first
command Peter taught the new church to obey.

Peter told the crowd to repent and be baptized because he was
obeying Jesus' command.

Let's Review...

Who is Jesus?

What is the church?

What did Jesus command the disciples?

How did the first churches obey?

What does it mean to repent?

Let's read Acts 3:19 aloud together.

> *Repent, then, and turn to God, so that your sins may be wiped
> out, that times of refreshing may come from
> the Lord. Acts 3:19*

When someone repents, they turn from their sin and turn

towards God. Typically, people choose their own way and walk away from God, which always leads to sin. People repent when they confess their sins, turn around, and walk towards God.

When we repent, we have the stain of our sins blotted out and God refreshes our life with his presence. Jesus is the Sunrise from on High and his church is the light of the world. So, believers should repent turning from darkness to the light.

Let's Review...

Who is Jesus?

What is the church?

What did Jesus command the disciples?

How did the first churches obey?

What does it mean to repent?

Why should we repent?

Let's read Matthew 11:20 aloud together.

> Then Jesus began to denounce the towns in which most of his
> miracles had been performed, because they did not repent.
> Matthew 11:20

After doing many miracles, Jesus denounced some of the towns he had visited for one reason: they refused to repent and turn back to God.

God wants to do a miracle in our heart and change us, but he asks us to turn from our sin and walk towards him. People who stiffen their neck or harden their heart find themselves under judgment.

Jesus is passionate about people repenting because he wants them to walk in the light. He wants to move among us.

Let's Review...

Who is Jesus?

What is the church?

What did Jesus command the disciples?

How did the first churches obey?

What does it mean to repent?

Why should we repent?

Who should repent?

Let's read Acts 17:30 aloud together.

> *In the past God overlooked such ignorance, but now he commands all people everywhere to repent. Acts 17:30*

This passage is a portion of Paul's message to the men of Athens. Paul was speaking to people who did not understand anything about Jesus. The Athenians had different opinions about how to live and what to believe.

Even wise philosophers like the men of Athens have no excuse because the time of ignorance is over. Now that Jesus has died as a sacrifice for the world, God expects people to repent of their sins and return to him.

Let's Review...

Who is Jesus?

What is the church?

What did Jesus command the disciples?

How did the first churches obey?

What does it mean to repent?

Why should we repent?

Who should repent?

How should we repent?

Let's read Acts 26:18 aloud together.

> 'To open their eyes and turn them from darkness to light, and from the power of Satan to God, so they may receive forgiveness of sins and a place among those who are sanctified by faith in me.' Acts 26:18

This verse is a wonderful description of what repentance looks like. Jesus spoke these words to Paul in a vision during his conversion. Repentance involves three points:

Ask God to open your eyes — When we repent, we ask God to

change our mind. We ask God to open our eyes to see our sin the same way that he sees it. We are blind to the truth and only God can help us see reality.

Turn from darkness to light — When we repent, we ask God to change our heart. We turn from the darkness to the light. We try to hide our evil deeds and thoughts, but God wants to heal us by bringing them into the light of truth so we will confess them.

Turn from the power of Satan to God —When we repent, we ask God to change our will. We turn from depending on the power of Satan to depending on the power of God. Instead of depending on our own efforts, we trust in God's unfailing grace.

When we repent, God promises he will forgive our sins. He holds none of the wrong things we have done before to our account. He changes our mind, our heart, and our will by his grace.

Let's Review...

Who is Jesus?

What is the church?

What did Jesus command the disciples?

How did the first churches obey?

What does it mean to repent?

Why should we repent?

Who should repent?

How should we repent?

What is the memory verse?

Let's read Mark 1:15 aloud together.

> *"The time is fulfilled, and the kingdom of God has come near. Repent and believe in the good news!" Mark 1.15 (IICSB)*

Everyone stands and says the memory verse ten times together. The first six times, they use their Bible or lesson notes. The last four times, they say the verse from memory. Learners say the verse reference before quoting the verse each time and sit down when finished.

Following this routine will help the trainers know what team has finished the lesson in the practice section.

Let's Review...

Who is Jesus?

What is the church?

What did Jesus command the disciples?

How did the first churches obey?

What does it mean to repent?

Why should we repent?

Who should repent?

How should we repent?

What is the memory verse?

Practice

Ask learners to divide into groups of four. If the large group has an odd number of people, one small group will have three members instead of four.

"Now we will practice the lesson to gain confidence so we can share it with friends and family. Jesus said to love God with all of your strength and practicing the lesson helps us do that. Teach the lesson to one another the same way we taught it to you. When you add a new question, practice repeating all the previous questions and answers, just as we did with you."

The first learner reads the first question, the group reads the scripture aloud, and the group answers the question. The first learner helps the group learn the hand motion (if there is one). The first learner reviews the answer. The second learner repeats this same process.

Copy this method as you go around your circle; each time add a question until the group can repeat the entire lesson together.

Finally, follow the directions for saying the memory verse together.

GROW

Goal

"Now we want to decide as a group how we will follow Jesus' command to repent. The first step is to identify the goal. In this case, our goal is to follow Jesus' command to repent. I will write 'Repent' at the top of the whiteboard or poster paper. That is our goal."

Write "Goal — Repent" at the top of the whiteboard or poster paper.

Roadblocks

"The next part of the grow process is to talk about roadblocks we face achieving the goal of following Jesus' command to repent, and helping others to obey this command. What are roadblocks people face when it comes to repentance? What are reasons people give for not repenting?

We will create a list of ten roadblocks. Some roadblocks we list may appear enormous, while others may seem small. Each person may also view the roadblocks differently. Share roadblocks, and I will write them down on the white board. We will stop when we have ten."

Write "Roadblocks" on the left side of the white board and number from one to ten. As learners share roadblocks, write them down.

Options

"Now that we have listed our goal and identified ten road-blocks keeping us from achieving our goal, we want to create a list of ten options of how we can overcome the roadblocks. Let's try to develop options that resolve as many roadblocks as possible."

Usually, groups come up with easier problem-solving ideas first and solutions that have already been tried.

"Let's keep in mind that some of our later ideas may be the best answers to the roadblocks we face. Share options, and I will write them down on the white board. We will stop when we have ten."

Write "Options" on the right side of the white board and number from one to ten. Record options as learners share them with the group.

What does God want?

"We have looked at our goal, the roadblocks preventing us from reaching our goal, and options for how we can overcome those roadblocks. The last part of the grow process is to decide as a group 'What does God Want?' Let us spend some time in prayer asking God to show us which option(s) we should follow to obey Jesus' command to repent. Someone please lead us in that prayer."

After time in discussion, ask the group to share which option they feel is best. Sometimes, the group can combine several options into one "What does God Want?" item. Record the goal in the Church Covenant Worksheet (found in the Resource Section) with a short description of how the group will obey the command on a practical level. At the end of the training sessions, each group member will sign the church covenant in a special ceremony if the group believes they are ready to become a church.

3

BELIEVE

I believe in Christianity as I believe the sun has risen: Not only because I see it,
but because by it I see everything else.
—C. S. Lewis

Learners can expect the following results in this lesson:

- Discuss the connection between Jesus as the chief cornerstone and the church as his building
- Understand how to obey Jesus' command to believe
- Memorize Romans 10:9
- Practice training one another using the "Believe" lesson
- Use the grow process as a group to decide how to obey Jesus' command to believe

Worship

Sing two choruses or hymns together.

Prayer

Ask the group to divide into pairs.

Share prayer concerns you have and pray for each other. Also, pray for our study time that God would lead and direct us according to his will.

Study

Who is Jesus?

Let's read 1 Peter 2:6 aloud together.

> *For in Scripture it says:*
> *"See, I lay a stone in Zion,*
> *a chosen and precious cornerstone,*
> *and the one who trusts in him*
> *will never be put to shame." 1 Peter 2:6*

Isaiah wrote this prophecy about Jesus six-hundred years before he came to earth. Jesus is the chief cornerstone—chosen and precious. Whoever believes in Jesus will never be put to shame.

Builders place every stone in a building referring to the cornerstone. Every stone depends on the cornerstone to be correct. Similarly, Jesus alone is the one every believer looks to for life and guidance.

Let's Review...

Who is Jesus?

What is the church?

Let's read 1 Peter 2:5 aloud together.

> *You also, like living stones, are being built into a spiritual house*
> *to be a holy priesthood, offering spiritual sacrifices acceptable to*
> *God through Jesus Christ. 1 Peter 2:5*

Jesus builds his church with living stones—people who have confessed that Jesus is the Christ, the Son of the living God.

Jesus is the Cornerstone and the Church is a Spiritual House

We obey Jesus' command to believe and build our house around the chief cornerstone

Jesus is the Cornerstone and the Church is a Spiritual House. We obey Jesus' command to believe and build our house around the chief cornerstone.

Jesus builds a spiritual house
for the living stones who bring people to God's presence—the role of a holy priesthood. This spiritual house made of living stones offers sacrifices to God because of what Jesus did on the cross.

Why is this important?

Take 5 minutes and discuss why it is important to know that Jesus is the cornerstone and the church are living stones.

- Jesus is the foundation; we base everything on him.

- Jesus is the chosen one; God has chosen us because Jesus died for us on the cross.
- Jesus is precious; we join him in reconnecting people to the living God.

Let's Review...

Who is Jesus?

What is the church?

What did Jesus command the disciples?

Let's read John 14:1 aloud together.

> *"Do not let your hearts be troubled. You believe in God; believe also in me." John 14:1*

Jesus told the disciples not to let their hearts be anxious. They believed in God; they should believe in him.

He shared this with the disciples the evening of the last supper, when all of them could tell that a time of great difficulty loomed ahead.

> *Believe – Cross your hands over your heart and then lift your hands in worship.*

Let's Review...

Who is Jesus?

What is the church?

What did Jesus command the disciples?

How did the first churches obey?

Let's read Acts 16:31 aloud together.

> *They replied, "Believe in the Lord Jesus, and you will be*
> *saved—you and your household." Acts 16:31*

The first churches called people to believe in the Lord Jesus Christ so they and the people in their household could receive everlasting life.

Let's Review...

Who is Jesus?

What is the church?

What did Jesus command the disciples?

How did the first churches obey?

What does it mean to believe in Jesus?

Let's read John 6:69 aloud together.

> *"We have come to believe and to know that you are the Holy*
> *One of God." John 6:69*

Let's read Matthew 16:16 aloud together.

> *Simon Peter answered, "You are the Christ, the Son of the living*
> *God." Matthew 16:16 (NASB)*

Peter confessed his belief and certainty that Jesus was the Christ, the Son of God.

When you believe in Jesus, you place your trust in him and make these two confessions, as well.

First, you believe that Jesus is the only way a person can have their sins forgiven and return to God. He is the Christ.

Second, you believe that Jesus is the Son of God—fully man and fully God. He was not just a good man or good teacher. He was not solely divine—unable to understand the suffering that every person faces. Jesus was fully God and fully man—able to save us from our sins and understand our condition.

Jesus is the chief cornerstone: the focus of everything the church does. We are the living stones—we believe and know that Jesus is the Christ, the Son of the living God. Jesus continues to build his church with these kinds of stones.

Let's Review...

Who is Jesus?

What is the church?

What did Jesus command the disciples?

How did the first churches obey?

What does it mean to believe in Jesus?

Why should we believe in Jesus?

Let's read 1 John 5:13 aloud together.

> *I write these things to you who believe in the name of the Son of*
> *God so that you may know that you have eternal life.*
> *1 John 5:13*

God has given us the Bible so we can know for sure that we have everlasting life. We have eternal life by believing in the name of the Son of God—Jesus.

Let's Review...

Who is Jesus?

What is the church?

What did Jesus command the disciples?

How did the first churches obey?

What does it mean to believe in Jesus?

Why should we believe in Jesus?

Who can believe in Jesus?

Let's read John 3:16 aloud together.

> *For God so loved the world that he gave his one and only Son,*
> *that whoever believes in him shall not perish but have eternal*
> *life. John 3:16*

God loved the world so much that he gave us his only Son.

No one who believes in Jesus will perish. God has given them the gift of everlasting life. God has opened his heart to every living person on the earth. That is good news!

Let's Review...

Who is Jesus?

What is the church?

What did Jesus command the disciples?

How did the first churches obey?

What does it mean to believe in Jesus?

Why should we believe in Jesus?

Who can believe in Jesus?

How should we believe in Jesus?

Let's read Romans 10:9–10 aloud together.

> *If you declare with your mouth, "Jesus is Lord," and believe in your heart that God raised him from the dead, you will be saved.*
>
> *For it is with your heart that you believe and are justified, and it is with your mouth that you profess your faith and are saved.*
> *Romans 10:9–10*

Believing in Jesus involves both a private confession and a public demonstration.

In the privacy of our heart, we believe that God raised Jesus from the dead—that Jesus is the Christ, the Son of the living God—and put our trust in him.

In public, we confess that Jesus is Lord to those around us and proclaim our loyalty to him.

Let's Review...

Who is Jesus?

What is the church?

What did Jesus command the disciples?

How did the first churches obey?

What does it mean to believe in Jesus?

Why should we believe in Jesus?

Who can believe in Jesus?

How should we believe in Jesus?

What is the memory verse?

Let's read Romans 10:9 aloud together.

> *If you declare with your mouth, "Jesus is Lord," and believe in your heart that God raised him from the dead, you will be saved. Romans 10:9*

Everyone stands and says the memory verse ten times together. The first six times, they use their Bible or lesson notes. The last four times, they say the verse from memory.

Learners say the verse reference before quoting the verse each time and sit down when finished.

Following this routine will help the trainers know what team has finished the lesson in the practice section.

Let's Review...

Who is Jesus?

What is the church?

What did Jesus command the disciples?

How did the first churches obey?

What does it mean to believe in Jesus?

Why should we believe in Jesus?

Who should believe in Jesus?

How should we believe in Jesus?

What is the memory verse?

Practice

Ask learners to divide into groups of four. If the large group has an odd number of people, one small group will have three members instead of four.

"Now we will practice the lesson to gain confidence so we can share it with friends and family. Jesus said to love God with all of your strength and practicing the lesson helps us do that. Teach the lesson to one another the same way we taught it to you. When you add a new question, practice repeating all the previous questions and answers, just as we did with you."

The first learner reads the first question, the group reads the scripture aloud, and the group answers the question. The first learner helps the group learn the hand motion (if there is one). The first learner reviews the answer. The second learner repeats this same process.

Copy this method as you go around your circle; each time add a question until the group can repeat the entire lesson together.

Finally, follow the directions for saying the memory verse together.

GROW

Goal

"Now we want to decide as a group how we will follow Jesus' command to believe. The first step is to identify the goal. In this case, our goal is to follow Jesus' command to believe. I will write, 'Believe' at the top of the whiteboard or poster paper. That is our goal."

Write "Goal — Believe" at the top of the whiteboard or poster paper.

Roadblocks

"The next part of the grow process is to talk about roadblocks we face achieving the goal of obeying the command of Jesus to believe and helping others to obey this command. What are roadblocks that keep people from believing in Jesus and receiving everlasting life in your culture, church, or situation?

We will create a list of ten roadblocks. Some roadblocks we list may appear enormous, while others may seem small. Each person may also view the roadblocks differently. Share roadblocks, and I will write them down on the white board. We will stop when we have ten."

Write "Roadblocks" on the left side of the white board and number from one to ten. As learners share roadblocks, write them down.

Options

"Now that we have listed our goal and identified ten roadblocks keeping us from achieving it, we want to create a list of ten options of how we can overcome the roadblocks. Let's try to develop options that resolve as many roadblocks as possible."

Usually, groups come up with easier problem-solving ideas first and solutions that have already been tried.

"Let's keep in mind that some of our later ideas may be the best answers to the roadblocks we face. Share options, and I will write them down on the white board. We will stop when we have ten."

Write "Options" on the right side of the white board and number from one to ten. Record options as learners share them with the group.

What does God want?

"We have looked at our goal of obeying the command of Jesus to believe, the roadblocks preventing us from reaching our goal, and options for how we can overcome those roadblocks. The last part of the grow process is to decide as a group 'What does God Want?' Let us spend some time in prayer asking God to show us which option we should follow. Someone please lead us in that prayer."

After time in discussion, ask the group to share which option they feel is best. Sometimes, the group can combine several options into one "What does God Want?" item. Record the goal in the Church Covenant Worksheet (found in the Resource Section) with a short description of how the group will obey the command on a practical level. At the end of the training sessions, each group member will sign the church covenant in a special ceremony if the group believes they are ready to become a church.

4

BAPTIZE

*We may never be martyrs but we can die to self, to sin, to the world, to our plans
and ambitions. That is the significance of baptism; we died
with Christ and rose to new life.*
—Vance Havner

Learners can expect the following results in this lesson:

- Discuss the connection between Jesus, the bride-
  groom, and the church, his bride
- Understand how to obey Jesus' command to baptize
- Memorize Romans 6:4
- Practice training one another using the "Baptize" lesson
- Use the grow process as a group to decide how to
  obey Jesus' command to baptize

Worship

Sing two choruses or hymns together.

Prayer

Ask the group to divide into pairs.

Share prayer concerns you have and pray for each other. Also, pray for our study time that God would lead and direct us according to his will.

Study

Who is Jesus?

Let's read Luke 5:34–35 aloud together.

> *Jesus responded, "Do wedding guests fast while celebrating with the groom? Of course not. But someday the groom will be taken away from them, and then they will fast." Luke 5:34–35 (NLT)*

The Pharisees asked Jesus why he and his disciples did not fast like John the Baptist and his disciples. Jesus responded to their question saying the bridegroom's friends don't fast when he is with them.

Jesus is the bridegroom. He loves the church and waits expectantly until the day he can wed his bride.

Let's Review...

Who is Jesus?

What is the church?

Let's read Revelation 19:7–8 aloud together.

Let us rejoice and be glad
and give him glory!
For the wedding of the Lamb has come,
and his bride has made herself ready.
Fine linen, bright and clean,
was given her to wear."
(Fine linen stands for the righteous acts of
God's holy people.) Revelation 19:7–8

In this passage, the heavenly choir is rejoicing in the coming reign of the Lord Jesus, the Lamb. The church is the holy bride of Christ. Beautifully clothed in bright, pure, fine linen. The fine linen is the righteous acts of the saints throughout time. When believers do good deeds, it adds to the glory and beauty of the bride of Christ—the church.

Jesus is the Bridegroom and the Church is His Bride

We obey Jesus' command to Baptize to show our commitment to Him

> Jesus is the Bridegroom and the Church is His Bride. We obey Jesus' command to Baptize to show our commitment to Him.

Why is this important?

Take 5 minutes and discuss why it is important to know that Jesus is the bridegroom and the church is his bride.

- Jesus loves his bride and wants to be with her.
- Jesus has chosen the church to have a unique relationship with him that no other group on earth enjoys.
- The church is to be spotless and holy, doing good deeds to present ourselves to Jesus as his beautiful bride.

Let's Review...

Who is Jesus?

What is the church?

What did Jesus command the disciples?

Let's read Matthew 28:19 aloud together.

Therefore, go and make disciples of all nations, baptizing them in the name of the Father and of the Son and of the Holy Spirit.
Matthew 28:19

Jesus commanded the disciples to baptize new believers.

Jesus gave this command to every believer in the Great Commission.

Baptize – Hold elbow of right arm with left hand. Move right arm down to the right side, and then move back up to the starting position, mirroring the motion of baptism.

Let's Review...

Who is Jesus?

What is the church?

What did Jesus command the disciples?

How did the first churches obey?

Let's read Acts 2:38 aloud together.

Peter replied, "Repent and be baptized, every one of you, in the name of Jesus Christ for the forgiveness of your sins. And you will receive the gift of the Holy Spirit." Acts 2:38

When Peter's sermon convicted the people of their sins, they asked Peter what they should do. He told them to repent and receive baptism in the name of Jesus Christ for the forgiveness of sins.

Peter and the other Apostles obeyed Jesus' command to baptize.

Let's Review...

Who is Jesus?

What is the church?

What did Jesus command the disciples?

How did the first churches obey?

What are three levels of authority in a church?

Many times baptism has caused controversy in the church. The three levels of authority will help explain how we can obey Jesus' command to baptize.

Let's read Ephesians 2:20–21 aloud together.

Built on the foundation of the Apostles and prophets, with Christ Jesus himself as the chief cornerstone. In him, the whole building is joined together and rises to become a holy temple in the Lord. Ephesians 2:20–21

First Level — Jesus

We do not vote on these, we only obey.

Examples: pray, give, forgive, repent, baptize…

Jesus' commands are universal and apply in every culture and every time.

Jesus

Apostles

Early Church

Church Tradition

Second Level — The Apostle's Commands

The Apostle's commands clarify Jesus' commands for particular cultural contexts. The church should consider the culture and time they were given when they interpret these commands.

We do not vote on the Apostle's commands because the Holy Spirit inspired the Apostles and these commands are God's word.

Third Level — New Testament Church Practices

The second level of authority are the practices of the New Testament. Unlike the commands of Christ and the Apostles, each church must decide if they will follow Early Church practice or not.

Examples: give all that you have for the church to share with others, baptize immediately, take the Lord's Supper every time you meet, etc.

Since Peter, Paul, and other New Testament believers practiced them, we should not forbid those who want to do the same. Every church must decide as a body of believers what New Testament practices it will keep or discard.

Fourth Level — Church History

Church traditions are practices the church has adopted since New Testament times. Each church must decide which traditions from church history they believe God wants them to follow. Scripture does not command these practices and churches should evaluate each one regularly to decide if it is still helpful.

Examples: Lord's Supper once a month, Wednesday night prayer meeting, wearing a suit in the pulpit, wanting people to attend a 6-month Bible study before receiving baptism...

If the tradition helps people follow Jesus, we should keep it. If the tradition hinders people from following Jesus, we should change it.

Let's Review...

Who is Jesus?

What is the church?

What did Jesus command the disciples?

How did the first churches obey?

What are three levels of authority in a church?

Why is it important to follow Jesus' commands?

Let's read Romans 6:16 aloud together.

> *Don't you know that when you offer yourselves to someone as*
> *obedient slaves, you are slaves of the one you obey—whether*
> *you are slaves to sin, which leads to death, or to obedience,*
> *which leads to righteousness? Romans 6:16*

Jesus has given us commands to guide us in our journey. When we obey his commands, we live his kind of life.

Let's Review...

Who is Jesus?

What is the church?

What did Jesus command the disciples?

How did the first churches obey?

What are three levels of authority in a church?

Why is it important to follow Jesus' commands?

What does baptism mean?

Let's read Romans 6:4 aloud together.

> *We were therefore buried with him through baptism into death in order that, just as Christ was raised from the dead through the glory of the Father, we too may live a new life. Romans 6:4*

Our baptism shows we have died to this world and have risen to a new life. God has done this because we have identified with what Jesus did through his crucifixion and resurrection.

Baptism is an outward picture of how God has changed our hearts. We publicly confess that just as Jesus died and rose again to walk in newness of life, so have we. Baptism means Jesus has changed us from the inside out.

Let's Review...

Who is Jesus?

What is the church?

What did Jesus command the disciples?

How did the first churches obey?

What are three levels of authority in a church?

Why is it important to follow Jesus' commands?

What does baptism mean?

Why is baptism important?

Let's read Galatians 3:27 aloud together.

> *And all who have been united with Christ in baptism have put*
> *on Christ, like putting on new clothes. Galatians 3:27 (NLT)*

Our baptism shows the world we have put on Christ.

We show the world that we have taken off our old sinful clothes and put on new holy clothes—clothes that imitate Jesus. We have a new nature. A new identity.

A bride puts on a new white dress to show her pledge to the bridegroom. In the same way, we are baptized to show our commitment to Jesus.

Let's Review...

Who is Jesus?

What is the church?

What did Jesus command the disciples?

How did the first churches obey?

What are three levels of authority in a church?

Why is it important to follow Jesus' commands?

What does baptism mean?

Why is baptism important?

Who should be baptized?

Let's read Acts 8:12 aloud together.

> *But when they believed Philip as he proclaimed the good news*
> *of the kingdom of God and the name of Jesus Christ, they were*
> *baptized, both men and women. Acts 8:12*

When Philip preached the good news, many men and women believed in Jesus and were baptized.

Like those men and women, any person who believes Jesus is the Savior and accepts the good news should receive baptism.

Let's Review...

Who is Jesus?

What is the church?

What did Jesus command the disciples?

How did the first churches obey?

What are three levels of authority in a church?

Why is it important to follow Jesus' commands?

What does baptism mean?

Why is baptism important?

Who should be baptized?

How should we baptize?

Let's read Mark 1:9–11 aloud together.

> *At that time Jesus came from Nazareth in Galilee and was baptized by John in the Jordan. Just as Jesus was coming up out of the water, he saw heaven being torn open and the Spirit descending on him like a dove. And a voice came from heaven: "You are my Son, whom I love; with you I am well pleased."*
> *Mark 1:9–11*

Jesus came from Nazareth and asked John to baptize him in the Jordan River. John immersed Jesus in the Jordan River. When Jesus came up out of the water, he saw the heavens parting in the Spirit descending on him like a dove. God said, "You are my beloved Son in whom I am well pleased."

We follow Jesus's example by practicing baptism by immersion.

The person performing the baptism typically will say, "I baptize you in the name of the Father, the Son, and the Holy Spirit. Buried in likeness with Jesus, raised in newness of life." Then, the person performing the baptism lowers the person into the water and raises him or her out of the water after a few seconds.

We encourage the witnesses present to applaud in approval or share a word of blessing over the baptized person.

Let's Review...

Who is Jesus?

What is the church?

What did Jesus command the disciples?

How did the first churches obey?

What does baptism mean?

Why is baptism important?

Who should be baptized?

How should we baptize?

What is the memory verse?

Let's read Matthew Romans 6:4 aloud together.

> *We were therefore buried with him through baptism into death in order that, just as Christ was raised from the dead through the glory of the Father, we too may live a new life. Romans 6:4*

Everyone stands and says the memory verse ten times together. The first six times, they use their Bible or lesson notes. The last four times, they say the verse from memory. Learners say the verse reference before quoting the verse each time and sit down when finished.

Following this routine will help the trainers know what team has finished the lesson in the practice section.

Let's Review...

Who is Jesus?

What is the church?

What did Jesus command the disciples?

How did the first churches obey?

What does baptism mean?

Why is baptism important?

Who should be baptized?

How should we baptize?

What is the memory verse?

Practice

Ask learners to divide into groups of four. If the large group has an odd number of people, one small group will have three members instead of four.

"Now we will practice the lesson to gain confidence so we can share it with friends and family. Jesus said to love God with all of your strength and practicing the lesson helps us do that. Teach the lesson to one another the same way we taught it to you. When you add a new question, practice repeating all the previous questions and answers, just as we did with you."

The first learner reads the first question, the group reads the scripture aloud, and the group answers the question. The first learner helps the group learn the hand motion (if there is one). The first learner reviews the answer. The second learner repeats this same process.

Copy this method as you go around your circle; each time add a question until the group can repeat the entire lesson together.

Finally, follow the directions for saying the memory verse together.

GROW

Goal

"Now we want to decide as a group how we will follow Jesus' command to baptize. The first step is to identify the goal. In this case, our goal is to follow Jesus' command to baptize. I will write, 'Baptize' at the top of the whiteboard or poster paper. That is our goal."

Write "Goal — Baptize" at the top of the whiteboard or poster paper.

Roadblocks

"The next part of the grow process is to talk about roadblocks we face achieving our goal of obeying the command of Jesus to baptize and helping others to obey this command. What are some roadblocks to baptizing people in your church, culture, or situation?

We will create a list of ten roadblocks. Some roadblocks we list may appear enormous, while others may seem small. Each person may also view the roadblocks differently. Share roadblocks, and I will write them down on the white board. We will stop when we have ten."

Write "Roadblocks" on the left side of the white board and number from one to ten. As learners share roadblocks, write them down.

Options

"Now that we have listed our goal and identified ten roadblocks keeping us from achieving our goal, we want to create a list of ten options of how we can overcome the roadblocks. Let's try to develop options that resolve as many roadblocks as possible."

Usually, groups come up with easier problem-solving ideas first and solutions that have already been tried.

"Let's keep in mind that some of our later ideas may be the best answers to the roadblocks we face. Share options, and I will write them down on the white board. We will stop when we have ten."

Write "Options" on the right side of the white board and number from one to ten. Record options as learners share them with the group.

What does God want?

"We have looked at our goal to obey the command of Jesus to baptize, the roadblocks preventing us from reaching our goal, and options for how we can overcome those roadblocks. The last part of the grow process is to decide as a group 'What does God Want?' Let us spend some time in prayer asking God to show us which option we should follow. Someone please lead us in that prayer."

After time in discussion, ask the group to share which option they feel is best. Sometimes, the group can combine several options into one "What does God Want?" item. Record the goal in the Church Covenant Worksheet (found in the Resource Section) with a short description of how the group will obey the command on a practical level. At the end of the training sessions, each group member will sign the church covenant in a special ceremony if the group believes they are ready to become a church.

5

MAKE DISCIPLES

Radical obedience to Christ is not easy... it is not comfort, not health, not wealth, and not prosperity in this world. Radical obedience to Christ risks losing all these things. But in the end, such risk finds its reward in Christ. And he is more than enough for us.
—David Platt

Learners can expect the following results in this lesson:

- Discuss the connection between Jesus as Commander and Chief and the church as his army
- Understand how to obey Jesus' command to teach others to obey his commands
- Draw your own discipleship web
- Memorize Matthew 28:19, 20
- Practice training one another using the "Make Disciples" lesson
- Use the grow process as a group to decide how to obey Jesus' command to teach others to obey his

commands

Worship

Sing two choruses or hymns together.

Prayer

Ask the group to divide into pairs.

Share prayer concerns you have and pray for each other. Also, pray for our study time that God would lead and direct us according to his will.

Study

Who is Jesus?

Let's read Revelation 19:11–13 aloud together.

> *Then I saw heaven opened, and there was a white horse. Its rider is called Faithful and True, and He judges and makes war in righteousness. His eyes were like a fiery flame, and many crowns were on His head. He had a name written that no one knows except Himself. He wore a robe stained with blood, and His name is the Word of God.*
> *Revelation 19:11–13 (HCSB)*

John saw the heavens opened in his vision and Jesus riding on a white horse, leading the armies of God. Jesus judges righteously and makes war on the enemies of God. His eyes are as a flame of fire; he wears many crown; and he is clothed with a robe sprinkled with blood.

Jesus is the Commander and Chief of God's army. Jesus has all power and authority to overcome his enemies.

Let's Review...

Who is Jesus?

Jesus is the Commander and Chief and the Church is His army

What is the church?

Let's read 2 Timothy 2:3–4 aloud together.

> *Endure suffering along with me, as a good soldier of Christ*
> *Jesus. Soldiers do not get tied up in the affairs of civilian life,*
> *for then they cannot please the officer who enlisted them.*
> *2 Timothy 2:3–4 (NLT)*

Paul writes Timothy reminding him that part of following Jesus is enduring hardship as a good soldier. Believers are soldiers in God's army and should be careful not to let earthly matters distract them from their mission.

Jesus' soldiers obey his commands and makes disciples who will also obey him.

Why is this important?

Take 5 minutes and discuss why it is important to know that Jesus is the Commander and Chief and the church is part of his army.

Jesus is the Commander and Chief and the Church is His army. Jesus' soldiers obey his commands and makes disciples who will also obey him.

- Jesus has a strategy to win the war against the forces of evil and the church must follow his orders.
- Jesus wants us to recruit other followers who will obey Jesus as well.
- When Jesus, our Commander and Chief, gives the church an order, we should obey immediately, all the time, and from hearts of love.

Let's Review...

Who is Jesus?

What is the church?

What did Jesus command the disciples?

Let's read Matthew 28:19 aloud together.

> *"Therefore go and make disciples of all nations, baptizing them in the name of the Father and of the Son and of the Holy Spirit.*
> *Matthew 28:19*

Jesus told his disciples to make disciples of all nations. Jesus spoke this at the end of his ministry, so we know that it is important.

Make Disciples — Hold hands together as if you are reading a book. Move "The book" forward and backward from the left side to the right side as if you are training others to follow Jesus.

Let's Review...

Who is Jesus?

What is the church?

What did Jesus command the disciples?

How did the first churches obey?

Let's read Acts 2:42 aloud together.

> *They devoted themselves to the Apostles' teaching and to fellow-*
> *ship, to the breaking of bread and to prayer. Acts 2:42*

Let's read Acts 14:21 aloud together.

> *After preaching the Good News in Derbe and making many*
> *disciples, Paul and Barnabas returned to Lystra, Iconium, and*
> *Antioch of Pisidia. Acts 14:21 (NLT)*

The first churches continued steadfastly in the Apostles' teaching. The Bible says the Apostles taught and preached Jesus. Many people came to Christ and became disciples. So the Apostles followed Jesus' command to make disciples.

Let's Review...

Who is Jesus?

What is the church?

What did Jesus command the disciples?

How did the first churches obey?

How do we make disciples?

Let's read Matthew 28:19–20 aloud together.

> *Therefore go and make disciples of all nations, baptizing them*
> *in the name of the Father and of the Son and of the Holy Spirit,*
> *and teaching them to obey everything I have commanded you.*
> *And surely I am with you always, to the very end of the age."*
> *Matthew 28:19–20*

Teaching others to obey Jesus' commands is the essence of making disciples. We can tell the Apostles were teaching people to obey Jesus' commands because everything they did in the second chapter of Acts obeys a direct command of Jesus. Jesus directs his followers not to teach everything that he commanded, but to 'teach them to *obey*' everything that he commanded.

All the lessons in *Starting Radical Churches* teach learners the commands of Jesus. They also teach disciples how to obey the commands practically. A good start is obeying and teaching others the nine commands in this book!

Let's Review...

Who is Jesus?

What is the church?

What did Jesus command the disciples?

How did the first churches obey?

How do we make disciples?

What does Jesus promise to his disciples?

Let's read John 8:31–32 aloud together.

> To the Jews who had believed him, Jesus said, "If you hold to my teaching, you are really my disciples. Then you will know the truth, and the truth will set you free." John 8:31–32

Jesus says that we are his disciples if we hold to his teaching. Again this tie in—that a disciple obeys Jesus' teaching. The wonderful promise is we will know the truth and the truth will set us free. He will set us free from the sin that entangles our lives.

Let's Review...

Who is Jesus?

What is the church?

What did Jesus command the disciples?

How did the first churches obey?

How do we make disciples?

What did Jesus promise to his disciples?

What does it look like to make disciples?

Let's read 2 Timothy 2:1–2 aloud together.

> *You, therefore, my son, be strong in the grace that is in Christ Jesus. And what you have heard from me in the presence of many witnesses, commit to faithful men who will be able to teach others also.*
> *2 Timothy 2:1–2 (HCSB)*

Jesus modeled developing a few disciples who then developed more disciples. The Apostles followed Jesus in his method of reproducing disciples. Paul commands Timothy in the verses above to multiply disciple-making disciples. The illustration below shows what can happen if disciples are faithful to raise up new disciples who make disciples. One reason we are teaching you simple lessons is so you can be faithful in your disciple making. Discipleship is not just for the pastor, but Jesus commanded every Christian to make disciples.

Have the learners refer to the disciple-making tree below and have them take a moment to draw their own disciple-making tree or web. Ask the learners, "Who discipled you?" "Who are you discipling?" Who are the people you are discipling — discipling?"

The learner's disciple-making tree may look very different from the example below. Help them see the importance of 3rd and 4th generation disciples.

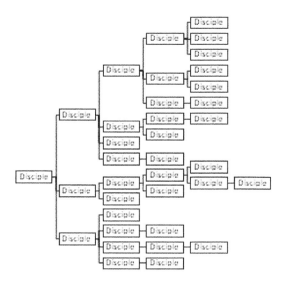

Let's Review...

Who is Jesus?

What is the church?

What did Jesus command the disciples?

How did the first churches obey?

How do we make disciples?

What did Jesus promise to his disciples?

What does it look like to make disciples?

What is the memory verse?

Let's read Matthew 28:19, 20 aloud together.

*Therefore go and make disciples of all nations, baptizing them
in the name of the Father and of the Son and of the Holy Spirit,
and teaching them to obey everything I have commanded you.
And surely I am with you always, to the very end of the age."
Matthew 28:19, 20*

Everyone stands and says the memory verse ten times together. The first six times, they use their Bible or lesson notes. The last four times, they say the verse from memory. Learners say the verse reference before quoting the verse each time and sit down when finished.

Following this routine will help the trainers know what team has finished the lesson in the practice section.

Let's Review...

Who is Jesus?

What is the church?

What did Jesus command the disciples?

How did the first churches obey?

How do we make disciples?

What did Jesus promise to his disciples?

What does it look like to make disciples?

What is the memory verse?

Practice

Ask learners to divide into groups of four. If the large group has an odd number of people, one small group will have three members instead of four.

"Now we will practice the lesson to gain confidence so we can share it with friends and family. Jesus said to love God with all of your strength and practicing the lesson helps us do that. Teach the lesson to one another the same way we taught it to you. When you add a new question, practice repeating all the previous questions and answers, just as we did with you."

The first learner reads the first question, the group reads the scripture aloud, and the group answers the question. The first learner helps the group learn the hand motion (if there is one). The first learner reviews the answer. The second learner repeats this same process.

Copy this method as you go around your circle; each time add a question until the group can repeat the entire lesson together.

Finally, follow the directions for saying the memory verse together.

GROW

Goal

"Now we want to decide as a group how we will follow Jesus' command to teach others to obey his commands. The first step is to identify the goal. In this case, our goal is to follow

Jesus' command to 'Make Disciples' and teach others to make disciples. That is our goal."

Write "Goal — Make Disciples" at the top of the whiteboard or poster paper.

Roadblocks

"The next part of the grow process is to talk about roadblocks we face achieving this goal of teaching others to obey Jesus' commands. What are roadblocks to teaching others to 'Make Disciples' in your culture, church, or situation? What are reasons we don't teach others to obey Jesus' commands?

We will create a list of ten roadblocks. Some roadblocks we list may appear enormous, while others may seem small. Each person may also view the roadblocks differently. Share roadblocks, and I will write them down on the white board. We will stop when we have ten."

Write "Roadblocks" on the left side of the white board and number from one to ten. As learners share roadblocks, write them down.

Options

"Now that we have listed our goal and identified ten roadblocks keeping us from achieving our goal, we want to create a list of ten options of how we can overcome the roadblocks. Let's try to develop options that resolve as many roadblocks as possible."

Usually, groups come up with easier problem-solving ideas first and solutions that have already been tried.

"Let's keep in mind that some of our later ideas may be the best answers to the roadblocks we face. Share options, and I will write them down on the white board. We will stop when we have ten."

Write "Options" on the right side of the white board and number from one to ten. Record options as learners share them with the group.

What does God Want?

"We have looked at our goal, the roadblocks preventing us from reaching our goal, and options for how we can overcome those roadblocks. The last part of the grow process is to decide as a group 'What does God Want?' Let us spend some time in prayer asking God to show us which option we should follow. Someone please lead us in that prayer."

After a time, ask learners to share which option they feel is best. Sometimes, the group can combine several options into one "What does God Want?" item. Record the goal in the Church Covenant Worksheet (found in the Resource Section) with a short description of how the group will obey the command on a practical level. At the end of the training sessions, each group member will sign the church covenant in a special ceremony if the group believes they are ready to become a church.

6

LOVE

It is an awesome, challenging thought. The Lord comes to us in our friends. What we do and are to them is an expression of what we are to him.
—Lloyd Ogilvie

Learners can expect the following results in this lesson:

- Discuss the connection between Jesus as the first-born and the church as his family
- Understand how to obey Jesus' command to love one another
- Memorize John 15:12
- Practice training one another using the "Love" lesson
- Use the grow process as a group to decide how to obey Jesus' command to love one another

Worship

Sing two choruses or hymns together.

Prayer

Ask the group to divide into pairs.

Share prayer concerns you have and pray for each other. Also, pray for our study time that God would lead and direct us according to his will.

Study

Who is Jesus?

Let's read Revelation 1:5 aloud together.

> *And from Jesus Christ, who is the faithful witness, the firstborn*
> *from the dead, and the ruler of the kings of the earth. To him*
> *who loves us and has freed us from our sins by his blood.*
> *Revelation 1:5*

Jesus is the faithful witness, the firstborn from the dead, and ruler over all earthly kings.

Jesus is the firstborn in God's family and our oldest brother.

Let's Review...

Who is Jesus?

What is the church?

Let's read Ephesians 2:19 aloud together.

> *So now you Gentiles are no longer strangers and foreigners.*
> *You are citizens along with all of God's holy people. You are*
> *members of God's family. Ephesians 2:19 (NLT)*

We are no longer strangers and foreigners but a part of God's kingdom and family.

Jesus is the oldest brother and the Church is His family.

We obey Jesus' command to love to follow His example and show the world we are His disciples.

God calls the church his family.

Jesus is the oldest brother and the Church is His family. We obey Jesus' command to love to follow His example and show the world we are His disciples.

Why is this important?

Take 5 minutes and discuss why it is important to know that Jesus is the firstborn and the church is his family.

- Jesus loves unity in his family—the church
- Jesus is the big brother the church wants to copy
- The family of God gives Jesus the highest honor because he is the firstborn and the beginning of God's family reborn.

Let's Review...

Who is Jesus?

What is the church?

What did Jesus command the disciples?

Let's read John 15:17 aloud together.

> *This I command you, that you love one another.*
> *John 15:17 (NASB)*

Jesus commanded his disciples to love one another. Our oldest brother wants everyone in the world to know his family loves one another.

> *Love – Clasp hands together as if you are shaking hands. Then, make a heart shape with both hands.*

Let's Review...

Who is Jesus?

What is the church?

What did Jesus command the disciples?

How did the first churches obey?

Let's read Acts 2:42 aloud together.

> *They devoted themselves to the apostles' teaching and to fellow-*
> *ship, to the breaking of bread and to prayer. Acts 2:42*

The first churches obeyed by sharing life together. We love one another when we fellowship—sharing our lives together as a family.

Let's Review…

Who is Jesus?

What is the church?

What did Jesus command the disciples?

How did the first churches obey?

What does it mean to fellowship?

Let's read Philippians 2:1–2 aloud together.

> *Is there any encouragement from belonging to Christ? Any*
> *comfort from his love? Any fellowship together in the Spirit?*
> *Are your hearts tender and compassionate? Then make me*
> *truly happy by agreeing wholeheartedly with each other, loving*
> *one another, and working together with one mind and purpose.*
> *Philippians 2:1–2 (NLT)*

We fellowship when we agree wholeheartedly, love one another, and work with one mind and purpose. Healthy families do all of these activities together.

Let's Review…

Who is Jesus?

What is the church?

What did Jesus command the disciples?

How did the first churches obey?

What does it mean to fellowship?

Why should we love one another?

Let's read 1 John 4:19 aloud together.

> *We love because he first loved us. 1 John 4:19*

Love comes from God because God is love. God showed us what love is by sending Jesus to die for us. We are able to love each other because the love of God is inside of us. God's love is the motivation for our loving each other.

Let's read John 13:35 aloud together.

> *"By this everyone will know that you are my disciples, if you love one another." John 13:35*

The world can tell we are disciples of Jesus because we love one another—we fellowship and share life together deeply. Loving one another is the true sign that we are genuine disciples. When the world sees the family of God loving one another, they believe that God sent Jesus.

Let's Review...

Who is Jesus?

What is the church?

What did Jesus command the disciples?

How did the first churches obey?

What does it mean to fellowship?

Why should we love one another?

Who is our example as we love one another?

Let's read John 13:34 aloud together.

> *"A new command I give you: Love one another. As I have loved*
> *you, so you must love one another."*
> *John 13:34*

Jesus commands every believer to love other believers. He commands us to love other Christians in the same way that he loves them. When we surrender to Jesus, his love flows out of our lives to brothers and sisters in fellowship.

Let's read Ephesians 5:2 aloud together.

> *And walk in the way of love, just as Christ loved us and gave*
> *himself up for us as a fragrant offering and sacrifice to God.*
> *Ephesians 5:2*

Jesus is our example. He loved us, so we love others. He sacrificed for us, so we sacrifice for others. When we love and sacrifice like Jesus, we offer a sacrifice to God the Father that is well pleasing. Jesus is our big brother and gives us the example to follow.

Let's Review...

Who is Jesus?

What is the church?

What did Jesus command the disciples?

How did the first churches obey?

What does it mean to fellowship?

Why should we love one another?

Who is our example, as we love one another?

How should we love one another?

Let's read Philippians 2:4–7 aloud together.

> *Do not merely look out for your own personal interests, but also for the interests of others. Have this attitude in yourselves which was also in Christ Jesus, who, although He existed in the form of God, did not regard equality with God a thing to be grasped, but emptied Himself, taking the form of a bond-servant, and being made in the likeness of men.*
> *Philippians 2:4–7 (NASB)*

Members of the family of God do not live their life with selfish ambition or conceit. Instead, they live a humble life and value others above themselves. We focus on helping others with their problems, rather than demanding everyone helps us with our problems.

Members of God's family have the same mindset as Jesus—our oldest brother. Although he was in his very nature God, he did not exalt himself, but humbled himself and became a servant for us. Families that practice sacrifice, honor, humility, and focus on the needs of others are safe places to grow and love.

Let's Review...

Who is Jesus?

What is the church?

What did Jesus command the disciples?

How did the first churches obey?

What does it mean to fellowship?

Why should we love one another?

Who is our example, as we love one another?

How should we love one another?

What is the memory verse?

Let's read John 15:12 aloud together.

> *My command is this: Love each other as*
> *I have loved you. John 15:12*

Everyone stands and says the memory verse ten times together. The first six times, they use their Bible or lesson notes. The last four times, they say the verse from memory. Learners say the verse reference before quoting the verse each time and sit down when finished.

Following this routine will help the trainers know what team has finished the lesson in the practice section.

Let's Review...

Who is Jesus?

What is the church?

What did Jesus command the disciples?

How did the first churches obey?

What does it mean to fellowship?

Why should we love one another?

Who is our example, as we love one another?

How should we love one another?

What is the memory verse?

Practice

Ask learners to divide into groups of four. If the large group has an odd number of people, one small group will have three members instead of four.

"Now we will practice the lesson to gain confidence so we can share it with friends and family. Jesus said to love God with all of your strength and practicing the lesson helps us do that. Teach the lesson to one another the same way we taught it to you. When you add a new question, practice repeating all the previous questions and answers, just as we did with you."

The first learner reads the first question, the group reads the scripture aloud, and the group answers the question. The first learner helps the group learn the hand motion (if there is one). The first learner reviews the answer. The second learner repeats this same process.

Copy this method as you go around your circle; each time add a question until the group can repeat the entire lesson together.

Finally, follow the directions for saying the memory verse together.

GROW

Goal

"Now we want to decide as a group how we will follow Jesus' command to love one another. The first step is to identify the goal. Our goal from this lesson is to obey Jesus' command to love one another. I will write, 'Love one another' at the top of the whiteboard (or poster paper). That is our goal."

Write "Goal — Love One Another" at the top of the whiteboard or poster paper.

Roadblocks

"The next part of the grow process is to talk about roadblocks we face achieving the goal of loving people and helping others to obey this command. What are some of the roadblocks to loving people in your church, community, or culture?

We will create a list of ten roadblocks. Some roadblocks we list may appear enormous, while others may seem small. Each person may also view the roadblocks differently. Share roadblocks, and I will write them down on the white board. We will stop when we have ten."

Write "Roadblocks" on the left side of the white board and number from one to ten. As learners share roadblocks, write them down.

Options

"Now that we have listed our goal and identified ten roadblocks keeping us from achieving our goal, we want to create a list of ten options of how we can overcome the roadblocks. Let's try to develop options that resolve as many roadblocks as possible."

Usually, groups come up with easier problem-solving ideas first and solutions that have already been tried.

"Let's keep in mind that some of our later ideas may be the best answers to the roadblocks we face. Share options, and I will write them down on the white board. We will stop when we have ten."

Write "Options" on the right side of the white board and number from one to ten. Record options as learners share them with the group.

What does God want?

"We have looked at our goal, the roadblocks preventing us from reaching our goal, and options for how we can overcome those roadblocks. The last part of the grow process is to decide as a group 'What does God Want?' Let us spend some time in prayer asking God to show us which option we should follow. Someone please lead us in that prayer."

After a time, ask learners to share which option they feel is best. Sometimes, the group can combine several options into one "What does God Want?" item. Record the goal in the Church Covenant Worksheet (found in the Resource Section) with a short description of how the group will obey the command on a practical level. At the end of the training sessions, each group member will sign the church covenant in a special ceremony if the group believes they are ready to become a church.

7

REMEMBER

We who have turned our lives over to Christ need to know how very much he longs to eat with us, to commune with us. He desires a perpetual Eucharistic feast in the inner sanctuary of the heart.
—Richard J. Foster

Learners can expect the following results in this lesson:

- Discuss the connection between Jesus as True Vine and the church as the branches
- Understand how to obey Jesus' command to observe the Lord's Supper
- Memorize First Corinthians 10:16
- Observe the Lord's Supper in a simple way that honors and glorifies Jesus
- Use the grow process as a group to decide how to obey Jesus' command to do this in remembrance of me

Worship

Sing two choruses or hymns together.

Prayer

Ask the group to divide into pairs.

Share prayer concerns you have and pray for each other. Also, pray for our study time that God would lead and direct us according to his will.

Study

Who is Jesus?

Let's read John 15:1 aloud together.

> *"I am the true vine, and My Father is the vineyard keeper".*
> *John 15:1(HCSB)*

Jesus is the true vine and his Father is the vineyard keeper.

Let's Review....

Who is Jesus?

What is the church?

Let's read John 15:5 aloud together.

> *"I am the vine; you are the branches. If you remain in me and I*
> *in you, you will bear much fruit; apart from me you can do*
> *nothing." John 15:5*

Jesus is the life-giving vine and we are the life-receiving branches. When we remain in him, we bear fruit. Apart from him, we can do nothing.

Jesus is the Vine and the Church are the branches.

We obey Jesus' command to remember his death on the cross to demonstrate He is the source of our life.

Jesus is the Vine and the Church are the branches. We obey Jesus' command to remember his death on the cross to demonstrate He is the source of our life.

Why is this important?

Take 5 minutes and discuss why it is important to know that Jesus is the true vine and we are the branches.

- Jesus is our source of spiritual life, we can do nothing apart from him.
- When we remain in Jesus, we produce fruit.
- We can trust Jesus as the true source of spiritual life and thank God that he has connected us to Jesus.

Let's Review....

Who is Jesus?

What is the church?

What did Jesus command the disciples?

Let's read Matthew 26:26–28 aloud together.

While they were eating, Jesus took bread, and when he had

*given thanks, he broke it and gave it to his disciples, say-
ing, "Take and eat; this is my body."*

*Then he took a cup, and when he had given thanks, he gave it
to them, saying, "Drink from it, all of you. This is my blood of
the covenant, which is poured out for many for the forgiveness
of sins." Matthew 26:26–28*

The night before his crucifixion, Jesus shared his last supper
with the disciples. Christians call this ceremony the Lord's
Supper and it is the highest form of Christian worship.

Jesus commanded his disciples to observe the Lord's Supper
as a remembrance of his death on the cross.

Remember — Put middle finger in the palm of the other hand
and repeat with the other hand (sign language for crucifixion)

Let's Review....

Who is Jesus?

What is the church?

What did Jesus command the disciples?

How did the first churches obey?

Let's read Acts 2:42 aloud together.

*They devoted themselves to the Apostles' teaching and to fellow-
ship, to the breaking of bread and to prayer. Acts 2:42*

The Apostles taught the Early Church to obey Jesus' commands, just as Jesus had commanded them in the Great Commission. The Early Church obeyed the command to repent

and believe. They obeyed the command to baptize. They obeyed the command to teach others to obey Jesus' commands. Loving one another characterized their lives in the first church.

They also taught the Early Church to obey Jesus' command to observe the Lord's Supper; 'the breaking of bread' refers to the Lord's Supper. The Apostles obeyed Jesus' commands and taught others to do the same. The Early Church did not follow "new" ideas of the Apostles, but the commands Jesus had taught them to follow.

Let's Review....

Who is Jesus?

What is the church?

What did Jesus command the disciples?

How did the first churches obey?

What does the Lord's Supper mean?

Let's read 1 Corinthians 11:23–26 aloud together.

> *For I received from the Lord what I also passed on to you: The Lord Jesus, on the night he was betrayed, took bread, and when he had given thanks, he broke it and said, "This is my body, which is for you; do this in remembrance of me."*

> *In the same way, after supper he took the cup, saying, "This cup is the new covenant in my blood; do this, whenever you drink it, in remembrance of me."*

*For whenever you eat this bread and drink this cup, you pro-
claim the Lord's death until he comes.*
1 Corinthians 11:23–26

Each part of the Lord's Supper has special meaning.

When Jesus took the bread, he gave thanks, broke it and said, "Take eat, and this is my body." The bread represents Jesus' body broken on the cross for our sins.

Then he took the cup, gave thanks, and gave it to them. He said, "Drink this cup because it is my blood of the new covenant." The cup represents Jesus' blood poured out on the cross to forgive our sins.

Let's Review....

Who is Jesus?

What is the church?

What did Jesus command the disciples?

How did the first churches obey?

What does the Lord's Supper mean?

Why is the Lord's Supper important?

Let's read I Corinthians 11:26 aloud together.

*For whenever you eat this bread and drink this cup, you pro-
claim the Lord's death until he comes. I Corinthians 11:26*

The Lord's Supper proclaims Jesus as Savior of the world on the cross. When we take the Lord's Supper, it reminds us and the world the price Jesus paid for our salvation.

Let's Review....

Who is Jesus?

What is the church?

What did Jesus command the disciples?

How did the first churches obey?

What does the Lord's Supper mean?

Why is the Lord's Supper important?

Who should take the Lord's Supper?

Let's read 1 Corinthians 11:27–29 aloud together.

> So then, whoever eats the bread or drinks the cup of the Lord in an unworthy manner will be guilty of sinning against the body and blood of the Lord.
>
> Everyone ought to examine themselves before they eat of the bread and drink from the cup.
>
> For those who eat and drink without discerning the body of Christ eat and drink judgment on themselves.
> 1 Corinthians 11:27–29

The apostle Paul directs believers about whom should take the Lord's Supper in the book of first Corinthians. Before we take the Lord's Supper, we should examine ourselves to make sure we are taking the supper in a way that honors Jesus' death on our behalf.

The Lord's Supper is not for unbelievers, but people who have repented and believed in Jesus as Savior. Believers celebrate what Jesus did on our behalf. The Lord's Supper is a holy time, so believers should make sure they have confessed their sins and are standing in right relationship with God before they take the Supper.

Let's Review....

Who is Jesus?

What is the church?

What did Jesus command the disciples?

How did the first churches obey?

What does the Lord's Supper mean?

Why is the Lord's Supper important?

Who should take the Lord's Supper?

How should we take the Lord's Supper?

Let's read I Corinthians 11:23–26 aloud together.

> *For I received from the Lord what I also passed on to you: The Lord Jesus, on the night he was betrayed, took bread, and when he had given thanks, he broke it and said, "This is my body, which is for you; do this in remembrance of me."*
>
> *In the same way, after supper he took the cup, saying, "This cup*

*is the new covenant in my blood; do this, whenever you drink it,
in remembrance of me."*

*For whenever you eat this bread and drink this cup, you pro-
claim the Lord's death until he comes. I Corinthians 11:23–26*

We observe the Lord's Supper the same way Jesus did with
his disciples. We share the Lord's Supper to remember Jesus'
death on the cross and the price he paid to restore us to God;
it reminds believers that Jesus has already paid the price for
our sin. We observe the Lord's Supper to honor and worship
the only one who could take away our sins—God's Son.

After we practice the memory verse together, we will share
the Lord's Supper together. We want to teach you a simple and
sincere way to observe the Lord's Supper anywhere.

Let's Review....

Who is Jesus?

What is the church?

What did Jesus command the disciples?

How did the first churches obey?

What does the Lord's Supper mean?

Why is the Lord's Supper important?

Who should take the Lord's Supper?

How should we take the Lord's Supper?

What is the memory verse?

Let's read 1 Corinthians 10:16 aloud together.

> *When we bless the cup at the Lord's Table, are not we sharing In the blood of Christ? And when we break the bread, are not we sharing in the body of Christ? 1 Corinthians 10:16 (NLT)*

Everyone stands and says the memory verse ten times together. The first six times, they use their Bible or lesson notes. The last four times, they say the verse from memory. Learners say the verse reference before quoting the verse each time and sit down when finished.

Following this routine will help the trainers know what team has finished the lesson in the practice section.

Let's Review....

Who is Jesus?

What is the church?

What did Jesus command the disciples?

How did the first churches obey?

What does the Lord's Supper mean?

Why is the Lord's Supper important?

Who should take the Lord's Supper?

How should we take the Lord's Supper?

What is the memory verse?

Practice

This practice session is different from the practice time in other sessions. Leaders of the group will show learners a simple way to share communion (Lord's Supper) together. This is a model that believers can use in almost any setting because it does not require expensive utensils.

Prepare the following before the session:

A plate — ask local believers to choose a plate used for special occasions in their culture. The plate can be gold or silver if available, but expense should not prevent people from sharing the Lord's Supper.

A cup — instead of using a separate cup for each person, this simple ceremony has only one cup. Participants should recognize the cup as one used for special occasions in their culture. The cup doesn't have to be gold or silver.

Bread — depending on your location, Lord's Supper wafers may be available. Many people, however, cannot afford and do not have access to store-bought wafers. Good alternatives include flat bread, crackers, or rice.

Grape juice or wine — depending on denomination and culture, some groups use wine while others prefer grape juice.

Arrange the elements on a small table in front of the person leading the ceremony. Some prefer to drape a white cloth on the table to make the event more formal.

Ask group members to gather for a celebration of the Lord's Supper. Some groups prefer to sit on the floor when they observe the Lord's Supper, while others sit in chairs.

Say the following:

"We want to share the Lord's Supper together. Jesus has given us this ceremony to remember his death on the cross. Because we are remembering God's Son giving his life for our sins, this is a holy time.

Let's spend a few moments preparing ourselves for the Lord's Supper. We will do this by examining ourselves and confessing to God any sins in our lives. Join me in a time of prayer and confession."

The group should pray silently while someone plays some worship music quietly in the background. If a musician is not available, consider playing a worship CD.

Don't rush the confession time. Allow the time necessary for the Holy Spirit to convict and cleanse people of their sin.

"Now that we have examined ourselves, let's celebrate the Lord's Supper together."

Take a piece of the bread and pass the plate to the person next to you. Ask them to take a piece of bread and pass the plate to their neighbor. Repeat giving and receiving the bread until every believer has a piece of bread.

Hold the bread up and say the following:

"This bread represents the broken body of Jesus for us. His body was broken on the cross when he died for our sins. He offered his body as a sacrifice for us. When we eat this bread, we are remembering the sacrifice of Jesus for us. Let's spend time in prayer thanking Jesus for sacrificing his body for us."

Ask someone in the group to say a prayer of thanksgiving to Jesus for giving his body sacrificially on the cross.

Hold the cup up and say the following:

"This cup represents the blood of Jesus poured out for our sins. Blood represents the life of a person and Jesus poured out his life on the cross for us. He died so we can have life. His blood gives us victory over our sins and over Satan. Let's spend time in prayer thanking Jesus for the power of his blood again sin and Satan."

Ask another person in the group to say a prayer of thanksgiving to Jesus shedding his blood on the cross for our sins.

Dip your piece of bread in the cup and say the following:

"We remember that Jesus' body was broken for us and that his blood cleanses us from all sin. We do this in remembrance of him. Lift the piece of bread soaked with wine to your mouth and reverently eat it in remembrance of Jesus."

Give the rest of the group the following directions:

"Let's continue in prayer and worship together. As God leads, come to the Lord's Supper table, dip your bread in the cup, and spend time in prayer thanking Jesus for his death on the cross. Do this in remembrance of him."

The group should pray silently until they feel led by God to take the Lord's Supper. While people are praying and celebrating the supper, someone plays worship music quietly in the background.

When everyone has finished taking the Lord's Supper, say the following:

"Jesus commanded us to observe the Lord's Supper, so today we have obeyed him and shown him how much we love him. Jesus enjoys sharing the Lord's Supper with his church. The Lord's Supper reminds us that Jesus is for us, in us, with us, and will never leave us.

When Jesus and the disciples finished the supper, they sang a worship song together. Let's do the same."

Close the ceremony singing a favorite worship song of the group.

GROW

Goal

"Now we want to decide as a group how we will follow Jesus' command to observe the Lord's Supper. The first step is to identify the goal. In this case, our goal is to follow Jesus' command to observe the Lord's Supper. I will write, 'Observe the Lord's Supper' at the top of the whiteboard or poster paper. That is our goal."

Write "Goal — Observe the Lord's Supper" at the top of the whiteboard or poster paper.

Roadblocks

"The next part of the grow process is to talk about roadblocks we face achieving the goal of observing the Lord's Supper and helping others to obey this command. What are roadblocks to celebrating the Lord's Supper in your culture, church, or situation?

We will create a list of ten roadblocks. Some roadblocks we list may appear enormous, while others may seem small. Each person may also view the roadblocks differently. Share roadblocks, and I will write them down on the white board. We will stop when we have ten."

Write "Roadblocks" on the left side of the white board and number from one to ten. As learners share roadblocks, write them down.

Options

"Now that we have listed our goal and identified ten road-blocks keeping us from achieving our goal, we want to create a list of ten options of how we can overcome the roadblocks. Let's try to develop options that resolve as many roadblocks as possible."

Usually, groups come up with easier problem-solving ideas first and solutions that have already been tried.

"Let's keep in mind that some of our later ideas may be the best answers to the roadblocks we face. Share options, and I will write them down on the white board. We will stop when we have ten."

Write "Options" on the right side of the white board and number from one to ten. Record options as learners share them with the group.

What does God want?

"We have looked at our goal, the roadblocks preventing us from reaching our goal, and options for how we can overcome those roadblocks. The last part of the grow process is to decide as a group "What does God Want?" Let us spend some time in prayer asking God to show us which option we should follow. Someone please lead us in that prayer."

After a time, ask the group to share which option they feel is best. Sometimes, the group can combine several options into one "What does God Want?" item. Record the goal in the Church Covenant Worksheet (found in the Resource Section) with a short description of how the group will obey the command on a practical level. At the end of the training sessions, each group member will sign the church covenant in a special ceremony if the group believes they are ready to become a church.

8

PRAY

Each time, before you intercede, be quiet first, and worship God in his glory.
Think of what he can do, and how he delights to hear the prayers of his
redeemed people. Think of your place and privilege in Christ,
and expect great things!
—Andrew Murray

Learners can expect the following results in this lesson:

- Discuss the connection between Jesus as the Great High Priest and the church as his temple
- Understand how to obey Jesus' command to pray
- Memorize John 16:24
- Practice training one another using the "Pray" lesson
- Use the grow process as a group to decide how to obey Jesus' command to pray

Worship

Sing two choruses or hymns together.

Prayer

Ask the group to divide into pairs.

Share prayer concerns you have and pray for each other. Also, pray for our study time that God would lead and direct us according to his will.

Study

Who is Jesus?

Let's read Hebrews 4:15 aloud together.

> For we do not have a High Priest who is unable to empathize with our weaknesses, but we have one who has been tempted in every way, just as we are—yet he did not sin. Hebrews 4:15

Jesus is our High Priest—the only one worthy to bring us to God. He became human so he could understand our temptations and struggles.

Let's Review...

Who is Jesus?

What is the church?

Let's read II Corinthians 6:16b aloud together.

For we are the temple of the living God.
As God has said:
"I will live with them and walk among them,
and I will be their God, and they will be my people."
II Corinthians 6:16b

The church is the spiritual temple of God—not a physical building. God has promised to dwell in us and walk with us. He is our God and we are his people.

Jesus is the high priest and the Church is His temple.

We obey Jesus' command to pray to join Him in interceding for the world.

> Jesus is the high priest and the Church is His temple. We obey Jesus' command to pray to join Him in interceding for the world.

Why is this important?

Take 5 minutes and discuss why it is important to know that Jesus is the High Priest and the church is his temple.

- Jesus is the holy one of God and he lives in us
- When we meet, God is with us and walks with us
- God is holy and wants his people to be holy

Let's Review...

Who is Jesus?

What is the church?

What did Jesus command the disciples?

Let's read Luke 18:1 aloud together.

> *Then Jesus told his disciples a parable to show them they should always pray and not give up. Luke 18:1*

Jesus shared a parable with his disciples to teach them they should always pray and not give up.

Pray — Form the classic "Praying hands" picture with your hands.

Let's Review...

Who is Jesus?

What is the church?

What did Jesus command the disciples?

How did the first churches obey?

Let's read Acts 2:42 aloud together.

> *They devoted themselves to the Apostles' teaching and to fellowship, to the breaking of bread and to prayer. Acts 2:42*

The first churches obeyed Jesus' command to pray. Many events in the book of Acts occur because people pray.

Peter prayed on the way to the temple and God healed a crippled man. Peter prayed on the rooftop and God showed him the Gentiles would receive the gospel. The church prayed and God delivered Peter from prison.

Paul and Silas prayed and God delivered them from prison with an earthquake. These accounts are only a few examples of how God's people prayed and God answered in the book of Acts.

Let's Review...

Who is Jesus?

What is the church?

What did Jesus command the disciples?

How did the first churches obey?

What is prayer?

Let's read Matthew 6:6 aloud together.

> *But when you pray, go into your room, close the door and pray to your Father, who is unseen. Then your Father, who sees what is done in secret, will reward you. Matthew 6:6*

Jesus said when we pray to go into our room, close the door, and pray to your Heavenly Father. God will see us praying in secret and reward us openly.

Prayer is a private conversation between you and your Father in heaven. During worship services, someone often prays on behalf of the entire church, but the usual practice of prayer is in private.

Let's Review...

Who is Jesus?

What is the church?

What did Jesus command the disciples?

How did the first churches obey?

What is prayer?

Why should we pray?

Let's read John 14:13 aloud together.

> *You can ask for anything in my name, and I will do it, so the*
> *Son can bring glory to the Father. John 14:13 (NLT)*

Jesus said we can ask for anything in his name. Jesus will answer our prayer so he can bring glory to his Father. We pray in Jesus' name so he will answer us and bring glory to his Father.

Let's Review...

Who is Jesus?

What is the church?

What did Jesus command the disciples?

How did the first churches obey?

What is prayer?

Why should we pray?

How did Jesus teach the disciples to pray?

Let's read Matthew 6:9–13 aloud together.

> *"Pray, then, in this way:*
> *'Our Father who is in heaven,*
> *Hallowed be Your name.*
> *Your kingdom come.*
> *Your will be done,*
> *On earth as it is in heaven.*
> *Give us this day our daily bread.*
> *And forgive us our debts [trespasses], as we also have forgiven*
> *our debtors [those who trespass against us].*
> *And do not lead us into temptation,*
> *but deliver us from evil.*
> *[For Yours is the kingdom and the power and the glory*
> *forever. Amen.']" Matthew 6:9–13 (NASB)*

Jesus taught the disciples to pray using an outline of prayer topics. We are going to learn about each topic and practice praying together.

Worship

"The first topic in prayer is worship. We pray, 'Our Father who is in heaven, hallowed be Your name.'

God is the Creator and the most-high God. He is worthy of worship and respect. When we come into his presence, our priority is to worship him.

Let's practice this topic of prayer using a hand motion to remember the prayer topic."

Worship – raise hands in praise to God.[1]

Ask the group to pray aloud with their hands raised in worship. Encourage them to practice praising God alone during their prayer.

Salvation for Others

"The second topic in prayer is praying that unbelievers will place their trust in Christ. We pray, 'Your kingdom come.'

God's kingdom comes to this earth as people leave the kingdom of darkness and enter the kingdom of light at salvation.

As we pray, ask God to save five people you know who are not believers. We know that God wants people to receive salvation, so you can know you are praying God's will when you ask for their salvation.

Let's practice this topic of prayer using a hand motion to remember the prayer topic."

Salvation for Others – cup hands and raise them as if asking for something.

Ask the group to pray aloud with their hands cupped to receive God's blessing. Encourage them to practice praying for the salvation of others alone during their prayer.

Obeying God's Word

"The third topic in prayer is obeying God's word. We pray, 'Your will be done on earth as it is in heaven.'

Obeying God's word brings life. Not following his word brings death. Many times, we find ourselves in a bad place because we are not obeying what God has told us to do.

During this topic of prayer, we search our hearts and confess any time we have not obeyed God's word. We pray for the strength to follow his word whatever the cost.

We also pray for others—they too will find the wonderful treasure of God's word in their life."

Obeying God's Word – raise hands in classic praying hands pose above your head—showing surrender.

Ask the group to pray aloud with their hands in the classic praying hands pose above their head. Encourage them to practice praying for themselves and others to obey God's word alone during their prayer.

Daily Needs

"The fourth topic in prayer is our daily needs. We pray, 'Give us this day our daily bread.'

God cares about our needs and wants to meet them. He wants us to talk to him about them so he can guide us and provide what we need.

During this topic of prayer, we ask God for all the things we need unashamedly. We know that he is the provider of every good and perfect gift. He owns the cattle on a thousand hills, and we need his help in our lives."

Daily needs — cup hands and raise them as if asking for something.

Ask the group to pray aloud with their hands cupped to receive God's blessing. Encourage them to practice praying only for their needs and the needs of others during the prayer.

Forgiveness

"The fifth topic in prayer is forgiveness. We pray, 'Forgive us our trespasses as we forgive those who trespass against us.'

Everyone needs forgiveness. In a fallen world, all of us wrong God and others. Without forgiveness, our sins would continue to mount and we would have no hope of freedom. Forgiveness, therefore, is an essential topic in prayer.

Jesus taught the disciples their willingness to forgive others had a direct effect on God's willingness to forgive them.

When we pray for forgiveness, we think of everyone who has wronged us who we have not forgiven. When we have our list, we forgive them. Then, we ask God to forgive our own list of sins."

Forgiveness — cross hands and push away while turning your head the opposite direction signifying repentance.

Ask learners to pray silently with their hands crossed, pushed away to the side, and head turned away as if they are turning away from their sin. Encourage them to practice asking and praying for forgiveness alone during their prayer.

Temptation

"The sixth topic in prayer is temptation. We pray, 'Lead us not into temptation, but deliver us from evil.'

Satan roams the earth as a roaring lion, seeking anyone he can devour. He most often devours people by tempting them to sin and watching with satisfaction when they fall.

Satan tempts some people with glory, so they want people to focus on them and their accomplishments.

Satan tempts others with gold, so they want to control as much money as possible, thinking this will give them security.

In the modern world, Satan tempts others with gadgets, so they have to own the latest technology, resulting in a cluttered rather than simple life.

Whatever the temptation, during this prayer topic, we ask God to lead us away from the temptation and deliver us from evil."

Temptation – cross hands and push away while turning your head the opposite direction signifying repentance.

Ask learners to pray silently with their hands crossed, pushed away to the side, and head turned away as if they are turning away from their sin. Encourage them to practice praying only about the items that tempt them during their prayer.

Surrender

"The seventh topic in prayer is surrender. We pray, 'For yours is the kingdom, and the power, and the glory, forever. Amen.'

We surrender to God and seek his kingdom first, knowing he will give us everything we need and more.

We surrender to God and depend on his power, knowing that without him we can do nothing.

We surrender to God and want him to be glorified, knowing that is the reason he created us.

During this topic of prayer, we concentrate on surrendering everything to God. Not building our own kingdom, but seeking and serving his kingdom alone. Not depending on our power, but resting in the power of the Holy Spirit. Not seeking reputation and status, but proclaiming his glory now and forever."

Surrender – raise hands in classic praying hands pose above your head–showing surrender.

Ask the group to pray silently with their hands raised in a classic praying hands pose above their head. Encourage them to practice praying only about surrendering to God's will during their prayer.

Let's Review...

Who is Jesus?

What is the church?

What did Jesus command the disciples?

How did the first churches obey?

What is prayer?

Why should we pray?

How did Jesus teach the disciples to pray?

What is the memory verse?

Let's read John 16:24 aloud together.

> *Until now you have not asked for anything in my name. Ask and you will receive, and your joy will be complete. John 16:24*

Everyone stands and says the memory verse ten times together. The first six times, they use their Bible or lesson notes. The last four times, they say the verse from memory. Learners say the verse reference before quoting the verse each time and sit down when finished.

Following this routine will help the trainers know what team has finished the lesson in the practice section.

Let's Review...

Who is Jesus?

What is the church?

What did Jesus command the disciples?

How did the first churches obey?

What is prayer?

Why should we pray?

How did Jesus teach the disciples to pray?

What is the memory verse?

Practice

Ask learners to divide into groups of four. If the large group has an odd number of people, one small group will have three members instead of four.

"Now we will practice the lesson to gain confidence so we can share it with friends and family. Jesus said to love God with all of your strength and practicing the lesson helps us do that. Teach the lesson to one another the same way we taught it to you. When you add a new question, practice repeating all the previous questions and answers, just as we did with you."

The first learner reads the first question, the group reads the scripture aloud, and the group answers the question. The first learner helps the group learn the hand motion (if there is one). The first learner reviews the answer. The second learner repeats this same process.

Copy this method as you go around your circle; each time add a question until the group can repeat the entire lesson together.

Finally, follow the directions for saying the memory verse together.

GROW

Goal

"Now we want to decide as a group how we will follow Jesus' command to pray. The first step is to identify the goal. In this case, our goal is to follow Jesus' command to pray. I will write, 'Pray' at the top of the whiteboard or poster paper. That is our goal."

Write "Goal — Pray" at the top of the whiteboard or poster paper.

Roadblocks

"The next part of the grow process is to talk about roadblocks we face achieving the goal of praying and helping others to obey this command. What are some of the roadblocks to prayer in your culture, church, or situation?

We will create a list of ten roadblocks. Some roadblocks we list may appear enormous, while others may seem small. Each person may also view the roadblocks differently. Share roadblocks, and I will write them down on the white board. We will stop when we have ten."

Write "Roadblocks" on the left side of the white board and number from one to ten. As learners share roadblocks, write them down.

Options

"Now that we have listed our goal of prayer and identified ten roadblocks keeping us from achieving it, we want to create a list of ten options of how we can overcome the roadblocks. Let's try to develop options that resolve as many roadblocks as possible."

Usually, groups come up with easier problem-solving ideas first and solutions that have already been tried.

"Let's keep in mind that some of our later ideas may be the best answers to the roadblocks we face. Share options, and I will write them down on the white board. We will stop when we have ten."

Write "Options" on the right side of the white board and number from one to ten. Record options as learners share them with the group.

What does God want?

"We have looked at our goal, the roadblocks preventing us from reaching our goal, and options for how we can overcome those roadblocks. The last part of the grow process is to decide as a group 'What does God Want?' Let us spend some time in prayer asking God to show us which option(s) we should follow to obey Jesus command to pray. Someone please lead us in that prayer."

After time in discussion, ask the group to share which option they feel is best. Sometimes, the group can combine several options into one "What does God Want?" item. Record how the goal in the Church Covenant Worksheet (found in the Resource Section) with a short description of how the group will obey the command on a practical level. At the end of the training sessions, each group member will sign the church covenant in a special ceremony if the group believes they are ready to become a church.

9

GIVE

You can give without loving. But you cannot love without giving.
—Amy Carmichael

Learners can expect the following results in this lesson:

- Discuss the connection between Jesus, Head of the body, and the church as the body of Christ
- Understand how to obey Jesus' command to give
- Memorize Acts 20:35
- Practice training one another using the "Give" lesson
- Use the grow process as a group to decide how to obey Jesus' command to give

Worship

Sing two choruses or hymns together.

Prayer

Ask the group to divide into pairs.

Share prayer concerns you have and pray for each other. Also, pray for our study time that God would lead and direct us according to his will.

Study

Who is Jesus?

Let's read Ephesians 4:15–16 aloud together.

> Instead, speaking the truth in love, we will grow to become in every respect the mature body of him who is the head, that is, Christ. From him the whole body, joined and held together by every supporting ligament, grows and builds itself up in love, as each part does its work. Ephesians 4:15–16

Jesus is Head of the church. He holds the church together and builds the church up in love as people do the tasks he has given them.

Let's Review

Who is Jesus?

What is the church?

Let's read 1 Corinthians 12:27 aloud together.

> Now you are the body of Christ, and individual members of it.
> 1 Corinthians 12:27 (HCSB)

The church is the body of Christ.

Jesus is the Head and the Church is His body.

We obey Jesus' command to _____
Give to supply everyone with   The church is the body of
the things they need to grow in   Christ. Jesus is the Head and the
Christ.   Church is His body.
_____

We are a part of his body as a whole, but also individual members.

Why is this important?

Take 5 minutes and discuss why it is important to know Jesus is Head of the church and the church his body.

- Jesus is the decision-maker and his body carries out his will.
- Jesus is the one who gives the power for the believers in his church to work together in love.
- Every member of the body is important and connected to Jesus—the Head of the body.

Let's Review

Who is Jesus?

What is the church?

What did Jesus command the disciples?

Let's read Luke 6:38 aloud together.

"Give, and it will be given to you. A good measure, pressed down, shaken together and running over, will be poured into your lap. For with the measure you use, it will be measured to you." Luke 6:38

Jesus commanded the disciples to give. He said to give in good measure, pressed down, shaken together, and running over. In the same way, we will receive after we give.

Those who give little, receive little. Those who give generously, receive generously.

Give — Place both hands at chest level and then motion outwards as if you are giving something to someone.

Let's Review

Who is Jesus?

What is the church?

What did Jesus command the disciples?

How did the first churches obey?

Let's read Acts 2:44–45 aloud together.

All the believers were together and had everything in common. They sold property and possessions to give to anyone who had need. Acts 2:44–45

The Apostles taught the first churches to obey Jesus' command to give. The believers shared everything they owned and sold their possessions to give to those in need.

Let's Review

Who is Jesus?

What is the church?

What did Jesus command the disciples?

How did the first churches obey?

What is the right way to give?

Let's read Matthew 6:1 aloud together.

> *"Be careful not to practice your righteousness in front of others to be seen by them. If you do, you will have no reward from your Father in heaven." Matthew 6:1*

When we give, we should be careful not to give to impress those around us. When we give to impress others, Jesus says we have our reward on earth and our Father will not reward us in heaven.

We give to bless others as God has blessed us, not to impress.

Let's Review

Who is Jesus?

What is the church?

What did Jesus command the disciples?

How did the first churches obey?

What is the right way to give?

Why should we give?

Let's read 1 John 4:19 aloud together.

We love because he first loved us. 1 John 4:19

Let's read Romans 8:32 aloud together.

He who did not spare his own Son, but gave him up for us all—how will he not also, along with him, graciously give us all things? Romans 8:32

When we give, we should remember that God has already given the greatest gift he could—his own Son. If he gave us his Son, then we can be sure that he will give us the other things that we need, as well. We love because he first loved us. We give because he first gave to us.

Some people have a mistaken picture of God. They believe he is miserly and gives only when we have begged and pleaded for a long time. In truth, however, God is a generous God—he proved this at the cross by giving us his Son.

Let's Review

Who is Jesus?

What is the church?

What did Jesus command the disciples?

How did the first churches obey?

What is the right way to give?

Why should we give?

Who should give?

Let's read 2 Corinthians 9:7 aloud together.

> *Each of you should give what you have decided in your heart to*
> *give, not reluctantly or under compulsion,*
> *for God loves a cheerful giver.*
> *2 Corinthians 9:7*

We should give from a cheerful heart. God loves to see his children give with joy in their heart. The person with a cheerful heart should give.

When we give to God, we should decide the amount by listening to our heart, not the convincing words of someone else. We should not give from a heart that does not want to give or give because someone has manipulated us into giving.

Let's Review

Who is Jesus?

What is the church?

What did Jesus command the disciples?

How did the first churches obey?

What is the right way to give?

Why should we give?

Who should give?

How should we give?

Let's read 2 Corinthians 9:6 aloud together.

> *Remember this: Whoever sows sparingly will also reap sparingly, and whoever sows generously will also reap generously.*
> *2 Corinthians 9:6*

We reap what we sow; if we give generously, God will bless generously. If we give like a miser, God will give to us in the same way.

Being generous does not depend on the amount. Jesus pointed to a widow giving two mites in the temple as the most generous giver that day. Even though her gift was significantly smaller than the rich people, she gave the most according to Jesus.

Let's Review

Who is Jesus?

What is the church?

What did Jesus command the disciples?

How did the first churches obey?

What is the right way to give?

Why should we give?

Who should give?

How should we give?

What is the memory verse?

Let's read Acts 20:35 aloud together.

"In everything I did, I showed you that by this kind of hard work we must help the weak, remembering the words the Lord Jesus himself said: 'It is more blessed to give than to receive.'" Acts 20:35

Everyone stands and says the memory verse ten times together. The first six times, they use their Bible or lesson notes. The last four times, they say the verse from memory. Learners say the verse reference before quoting the verse each time and sit down when finished.

Following this routine will help the trainers know what team has finished the lesson in the practice section.

Let's Review

Who is Jesus?

What is the church?

What did Jesus command the disciples?

How did the first churches obey?

What is the right way to give?

Why should we give?

Who should give?

How should we give?

What is the memory verse?

Practice

Ask learners to divide into groups of four. If the large group has an odd number of people, one small group will have three members instead of four.

"Now we will practice the lesson to gain confidence so we can share it with friends and family. Jesus said to love God with all of your strength and practicing the lesson helps us do that. Teach the lesson to one another how we taught it to you. When you add a new question, practice repeating all the previous questions and answers, just as we did with you."

The first learner reads the first question, the group reads the scripture aloud, and the group answers the question. The first learner helps the group learn the hand motion (if there is one). The first learner reviews the answer. The second learner repeats this same process.

Copy this method as you go around your circle; each time add a question until the group can repeat the entire lesson together.

Finally, follow the directions for saying the memory verse together.

GROW

Goal

"Now we want to decide as a group how we will follow Jesus' command to give. The first step is to identify the goal. In this case, our goal is to follow Jesus' command to give. I will write, 'Give' at the top of the whiteboard or poster paper. That is our goal."

Write "Goal — Give" at the top of the whiteboard or poster paper.

Roadblocks

"The next part of the grow process is to talk about roadblocks we face achieving the goal to obey Jesus' command to give and helping others to obey this command. What roadblocks to giving do you face in your culture, church, or situation?

We will create a list of ten roadblocks. Some roadblocks we list may appear enormous, while others may seem small. Each person may also view the roadblocks differently. Share roadblocks, and I will write them down on the white board. We will stop when we have ten."

Write "Roadblocks" on the left side of the white board and number from one to ten. As learners share roadblocks, write them down.

Options

"Now that we have listed our goal to give and identified ten roadblocks keeping us from achieving it, we want to create a list of ten options of how we can overcome the roadblocks. Let's try to develop options that resolve as many roadblocks as possible."

Usually, groups come up with easier problem-solving ideas first and solutions that have already been tried.

"Let's keep in mind that some of our later ideas may be the best answers to the roadblocks we face. Share options, and I will write them down on the white board. We will stop when we have ten."

Write "Options" on the right side of the white board and number from one to ten. Record options as learners share them with the group.

What does God want?

"We have looked at our goal, the roadblocks preventing us from reaching our goal, and options for how we can overcome those roadblocks. The last part of the grow process is to decide as a group "What does God Want?" Let us spend some time in prayer asking God to show us which option we should follow. Someone please lead us in that prayer."

After a time, ask the group to share which option they feel is best. Sometimes, the group can combine several options into one "What does God Want?" item. Record the goal in the Church Covenant Worksheet (found in the Resource Section) with a short description of how the group will obey the command on a practical level. At the end of the training sessions, each group member will sign the church covenant in a special ceremony if the group believes they are ready to become a church.

10

WORSHIP

God is pursuing with omnipotent passion a worldwide purpose of gathering joyful worshipers for himself from every tribe and tongue and people and nation. He has an inexhaustible enthusiasm for the supremacy of his name among the nations.
—John Piper

Learners can expect the following results in this lesson:

- Discuss the connection between Jesus as the Good Shepherd and the church as his flock
- Understand how to obey Jesus' command to Worship
- Memorize John 4:23
- Practice training one another using the "Worship" lesson
- Use the grow process as a group to decide how to obey Jesus' command to Worship

Worship

Sing two choruses or hymns together.

Prayer

Ask the group to divide into pairs.

Share prayer concerns you have and pray for each other. Also, pray for our study time that God would lead and direct us according to his will.

Study

Who is Jesus?

Let's read John 10:11 aloud together.

> *I am the good shepherd. The good shepherd lays down his life*
> *for the sheep. John 10:11*

Jesus is the good shepherd. He cares for his sheep and guides them on the right path. We know how much he loves us because he laid down his life for us on the cross.

Jesus is the good shepherd, so we have everything we need in this life. Even in our darkest hour, Jesus walks alongside us and guide us to a quiet and restful place.

Let's Review...

Who is Jesus?

What is the church?

Let's read Luke 12:32 aloud together.

> *"Do not be afraid, little flock, for your Father has been pleased to give you the kingdom." Luke 12:32*

Jesus is the good shepherd, and he calls us his little flock. When Satan tempts us to be afraid, we should remember that God gives us his kingdom with joy and pleasure.

Jesus is the Good Shepherd and the Church is His flock.

We obey Jesus' command to worship because Jesus is the lamb slain for our sin.

_____

Jesus is the Good Shepherd and the Church is His flock. We obey Jesus' command to worship because Jesus is the lamb slain for our sin.

_____

A church is like a flock of sheep and looks to Jesus for direction and provision. Like a flock of sheep, we need to be careful not to stray from the shepherd, but follow him.

Why is this important?

Take 5 minutes and discuss why it is important to know that Jesus is the good shepherd and the church is his flock.

- Jesus leads; we follow him.
- Jesus provide; we look to him.

- Jesus protects; we trust him.

Let's Review...

Who is Jesus?

What is the church?

What did Jesus command the disciples?

Let's read John 4:24 aloud together.

> "For God is Spirit, so those who worship him must worship in
> spirit and in truth." John 4:24 (NLT)

Jesus said that God is Spirit. Those who worship God must worship him in Spirit and truth.

> *Worship — Lift your hands in worship.*

Let's Review...

Who is Jesus?

What is the church?

What did Jesus command the disciples?

How did the first churches obey?

Let's read Act 2:46–47 aloud together.

> *Every day they continued to meet together in the temple
> courts. They broke bread in their homes and ate together with
> glad and sincere hearts, praising God and enjoying the favor of*

> *all the people. And the Lord added to their number daily those*
> *who were being saved. So continuing daily with one accord in*
> *the temple, and breaking bread from house to house, they ate*
> *their food with gladness and simplicity of heart, praising God*
> *and having favor with all the people. And the Lord added to the*
> *church daily those who were being saved. Act 2:46–47*

The first church continued to worship in the temple every day. They also met in their homes with gladness and sincere hearts. Praising God and favor from men characterized their lives.

Let's Review...

Who is Jesus?

What is the church?

What did Jesus command the disciples?

How did the first churches obey?

What is worship?

Let's read Psalms 100:1–2, 4 aloud together.

> *Shout for joy to the Lord, all the earth. Worship the Lord with*
> *gladness; come before him with joyful songs. Enter his gates*
> *with thanksgiving and his courts with praise; give thanks to*
> *him and praise his name.*
> *Psalms 100:1–2, 4*

Worship is praising his name! We shout triumphantly to the Lord and come into his presence with joyful songs when we worship. We come before the living God with thanksgiving and worship for all he has done. We serve him with our lives and gladness, so worship is not only singing, but also the way we live our lives.

Let's Review...

Who is Jesus?

What is the church?

What did Jesus command the disciples?

How did the first churches obey?

What is worship?

Why should we worship?

Let's read Psalms 100:3, 5 aloud together.

> Know that the Lord is God. It is he who made us, and we are his; we are his people, the sheep of his pasture. For the Lord is good and his love endures forever; his faithfulness continues through all generations.
> Psalms 100:3, 5

We worship God because he made us and we are his sheep. We also worship him because of his great deeds and his goodness to us. God is good, his love is eternal, and he is faithful to every generation. He has also made us and made us his flock.

When we worship God in spirit, we connect with him as his people, his sheep, and his loved ones.

When we worship God in truth, we recognize who he is—his mighty power, and his faithful character.

Let's Review...

Who is Jesus?

What is the church?

What did Jesus command the disciples?

How did the first churches obey?

What is worship?

Why should we worship?

Whom do we worship?

Let's read Revelation 5:11–12 aloud together.

> *Then I looked and heard the voice of many angels, numbering thousands upon thousands, and ten thousand times ten thousand. They encircled the throne and the living creatures and the elders. In a loud voice they were saying:*
>
> *"Worthy is the Lamb, who was slain,*
> *to receive power and wealth and wisdom and strength*
> *and honor and glory and praise!" Revelation 5:11–12*

In his vision, the apostle John saw countless heavenly beings worshiping the Lamb of God—Jesus. We worship Jesus because he offered himself as a sacrifice for our sins. We worship the only one who is worthy of worship.

All of them proclaim with a loud voice that Jesus is worthy to receive the best gifts man can give. Jesus is worthy to receive all power, riches, wisdom, strength, honor, glory, and blessings. He deserves everything we can give.

Let's Review...

Who is Jesus?

What is the church?

What did Jesus command the disciples?

How did the first churches obey?

What is worship?

Why should we worship?

Whom do we worship?

How should we worship?

Let's read Colossians 3:16–17 aloud together.

> *Let the message of Christ dwell among you richly as you teach and admonish one another with all wisdom through psalms, hymns, and songs from the Spirit, singing to God with gratitude in your hearts. And whatever you do, whether in word or deed, do it all in the name of the Lord Jesus, giving thanks to God the Father through him. Colossians 3:16–17*

- We worship God when we let the word of Christ live richly in our lives.
- We worship God when we teach and encourage one another to follow Jesus.
- We worship God when we sing psalms, hymns, and

spiritual songs to God with thanksgiving.
- We worship God when we live our lives copying Jesus with a thankful heart to God.

Let's Review...

Who is Jesus?

What is the church?

What did Jesus command the disciples?

How did the first churches obey?

What is worship?

Why should we worship?

Whom do we worship?

How should we worship?

What is the memory verse?

Let's read John 4:23 aloud together.

> *But the time is coming—indeed it's here now—when true wor-*
> *shipers will worship the Father in spirit and in truth. The*
> *Father is looking for those who will worship him that way.*
> *John 4:23 (NLT)*

Jesus is letting us know that his entrance into the world brings this new time of worship. His worshipers must worship in the Spirit and in truth.

Everyone stands and says the memory verse ten times together. The first six times, they use their Bible or lesson notes. The last four times, they say the verse from memory. Learners say the verse reference before quoting the verse each time and sit down when finished.

Following this routine will help the trainers know what team has finished the lesson in the practice section.

Let's Review...

Who is Jesus?

What is the church?

What did Jesus command the disciples?

How did the first churches obey?

What is worship?

Why should we worship?

Whom do we worship?

How should we worship?

What is the memory verse?

Practice

Ask learners to divide into groups of four. If the large group has an odd number of people, one small group will have three members instead of four.

"Now we will practice the lesson to gain confidence so we can share it with friends and family. Jesus said to love God with all of your strength and practicing the lesson helps us do that. Teach the lesson to one another how we taught it to you. When you add a new question, practice repeating all the previous questions and answers, just as we did with you."

The first learner reads the first question, the group reads the scripture aloud, and the group answers the question. The first learner helps the group learn the hand motion (if there is one). The first learner reviews the answer. The second learner repeats this same process.

Copy this method as you go around your circle; each time add a question until the group can repeat the entire lesson together.

Finally, follow the directions for saying the memory verse together.

GROW

Goal

"Now we want to decide as a group how we will follow Jesus' command to worship in spirit and truth. The first step is to identify the goal. In this case, our goal is to follow Jesus' command to worship in spirit and truth. I will write, 'Worship in Spirit and Truth' at the top of the whiteboard or poster paper. That is our goal."

Write "Goal — Worship in Spirit and Truth" at the top of the whiteboard or poster paper.

Roadblocks

"The next part of the grow process is to talk about roadblocks we face achieving the goal of worshiping in spirit and truth and helping others to obey this command. What are roadblocks people face in your culture, church, or situation that prevent people from worshiping God in Spirit and in truth?

We will create a list of ten roadblocks. Some roadblocks we list may appear enormous, while others may seem small. Each person may also view the roadblocks differently. Share roadblocks, and I will write them down on the white board. We will stop when we have ten."

Write "Roadblocks" on the left side of the white board and number from one to ten. As learners share roadblocks, write them down.

Options

"Now that we have listed our goal of worshiping in spirit and truth and identified ten roadblocks keeping us from achieving it, we want to create a list of ten options of how we can overcome the roadblocks. Let's try to develop options that resolve as many roadblocks as possible."

Usually, groups come up with easier problem-solving ideas first and solutions that have already been tried.

"Let's keep in mind that some of our later ideas may be the best answers to the roadblocks we face. Share options, and I will write them down on the white board. We will stop when we have ten."

Write "Options" on the right side of the white board and number from one to ten. Record options as learners share them with the group.

What does God want?

"We have looked at our goal, the roadblocks preventing us from reaching our goal, and options for how we can overcome those roadblocks. The last part of the grow process is to decide as a group 'What does God Want?' Let us spend some time in prayer asking God to show us which option(s) we should follow. Someone please lead us in that prayer."

After a time, ask learners to share which option they feel is best. Sometimes, the group can combine several options into one "What does God Want?" item. Record the goal in the Church Covenant Worksheet (found in the Resource Section) with a short description of how the group will obey the command on a practical level. At the end of the training sessions, each group member will sign the church covenant in a special ceremony if the group believes they are ready to become a church.

CHURCH DEDICATION - GOD'S CHURCH

Toil together, fight, run, suffer, rest, and rise up together as God's stewards,
companions of his table, and his servants!
—Ignatius, letter to Polycarp, c. AD 120

In *Starting Radical Churches*, learners have explored the three pillars of a great church and nine basic commands of Christ the disciples taught the first churches to obey. They have studied nine biblical pictures of the relationship between Jesus and the church. Learners have also used the grow process after each lesson to decide how they as a group will obey the nine basic commands of Christ.

Now the disciple group needs to decide if God wants them to become a church. The last lesson is a covenant service for groups that decide that God has called them to start a church.

The covenant service includes a time of worship and prayer. Learners share testimonies about how God is moving in their group. They also recite the lessons they have learned from memory. Finally, the disciple group transitions to a church when they commit to follow Jesus' nine basic commands and sign the church covenant together. Some churches choose to observe the Lord's Supper or hold a baptismal service to end the covenant service.

Celebration

Worship

Before the covenant service, arrange for a group member to lead in two choruses or hymns to begin the covenant service.

Prayer

Before the covenant service, arrange for a group member to pray for God's presence and blessing during the covenant service.

Testimonies

Before the covenant service, arrange for two more people to share a short testimony during the service about how God has spoken to them during the training times.

Review

Before the covenant service, ask someone in the group to lead a review of the training lessons during the service.

The review person helps the group to recite the entire training by saying the lesson name. Then, they ask each question and lead the group in repeating the answers and hand motions. Finally, they ask the group to say the memory verse together.

Covenant

Group members take turns reading each commitment and scripture in the church covenant.

After they read the commitments and scripture, a recognized leader asks the group if they are ready to commit to becoming a church.

Are we ready as a group to become a church according to Jesus' commands?

If the group answers "Yes", the recognized leader affirms their choice, prays for the group, and asks each member to sign the church covenant as a sign of their commitment.

If the group answers "No," the recognized leader affirms their choice, prays for the group, and encourages the group to revisit the covenant as God leads.

End the covenant service with a time of worship, the Lord's Supper, or a celebration of baptism.

THANK YOU

Before you go, I'd like to say "thank you" again for purchasing my book and I hope you have been blessed by it. I know you could have picked from dozens of books, but you felt the Lord leading you to mine.

Again, a big thank you for downloading *Starting Radical Churches* and reading it to the end.

Could I ask a *small* favor? Please take a minute to leave a review for this book on Amazon?

Think of your brief review as giving a short testimony that helps others know if this book is what they need to grow in their spiritual life.

Click Here to Share a Review

Your review will help me continue to write Kindle books that help people grow in their walk with Jesus. And if you loved it, please let me know that too! :>

BONUS

Don't forget to download your free *Making Disciples Bonus Pak*!

The free *Making Disciples Bonus Pak* which includes three resources to help you pray powerful prayers:

- *100 Promises Audio Version*
- *40 Discipleship Quotes*
- *40 Powerful Prayers*

All are suitable for framing. To download your free *Making Disciples Bonus Pak*, CLICK HERE

I've also included an excerpt from my bestselling book *Powerful Prayers in the War Room*. God has blessed many through this book and I wanted to give you a chance to "try before you buy." To order *Powerful Prayers in the War Room*, CLICK HERE.

POWERFUL PRAYERS IN THE WAR ROOM

INTRODUCTION

The one concern of the devil is to keep Christians from praying. He fears nothing
from prayerless studies, prayerless work and prayerless religion. He laughs at
our toil, mocks at our wisdom, but he trembles when we pray.
– Samuel Chadwick

This is a simple book on prayer.

You will learn the most important lessons I've gathered about prayer in the last 40 years – principles I wish people had taught me long ago. I'm not as powerful a prayer warrior as I want to be, but the truths I will share with you have helped my prayer life a great deal. The lessons you will learn in this book have helped me, and I believe will help you, too.

For many years, prayer was frustrating and hard for me to do consistently. This was my problem: I wanted to pray, I had been told I should pray, but I didn't know how to pray. When I tried to pray my mind would wander, I found myself bored, and I felt prayer was a complicated exercise I could never master. Just being honest. Conversations with other believers convinced me I wasn't the only one feeling that way about prayer. Earnest followers of Jesus shared similar thoughts.

When our family of six moved to Southeast Asia as missionaries, spiritual warfare became a real issue. Having pastored in America, my prayer life had looked like a roller coaster – some highs, but mostly lows, twists, and turns. Working with national believers for twelve years overseas, I was struck with how they prayed powerful prayers and I didn't. I don't mean emotional prayers; I mean prayers that were answered in ways that brought glory to God and saw His kingdom advance on the earth.

So, I started a journey of learning how to pray. Although I read many books on prayer, my main strategy was to look in the Bible and see how Jesus prayed and what He prayed about during his ministry. Then, I tried to copy Him in a way that would forge a habit. The rest of the book outlines the helpful gems I learned: the four weapons of prayer, seven powerful prayer topics, four ways God answers prayer, three war room prayer strategies, and nine tips to improve your prayer life.

We need powerful prayer warriors in the war room if our world is going to change. Clearly, most of the problems the church faces today are from a lack of prayer. Use this book to learn how to pray better. Use it to teach your children and grandchildren. God has always used the simple things to confound the wise. My prayer is God would use me and you to change the world one more time. Change, I believe, will only come on our knees.

CHAPTER 1 – FOUR WEAPONS OF POWERFUL PRAYER

When the devil sees a man or woman who really believes in prayer, who knows how to pray, and who really does pray, and, above all, when he sees a whole church on its face before God in prayer, he trembles as much as he ever did, for he knows that his day in that church or community is at an end.
– R.A. Torrey

Many people struggle with knowing how to pray. I know I have through the years. They have heard many times they should pray, but never received the tools to do so. They enter the War Room of prayer empty-handed and soon grow discouraged. They find themselves wishing they could pray better and feeling guilty they don't.

As you enter the War Room, remember Jesus is with you. He is the Great High Priest and knows how to pray perfectly. During his ministry on earth, Jesus showed his disciples how to pray, and he wants to show you how to pray too. Few actions make Jesus happier than when one of his children bow beside him and join him in prayer!

In this section, you will learn four weapons of powerful prayer: praise, repentance, asking, and yielding. Each part is important to a healthy prayer life. If your prayer life is dry or boring, usually the reason is one of the four weapons of prayer is missing. Make each weapon of powerful prayer a habit and watch your prayer life grow.

Praise

> The right way to pray is to stretch out our hands and ask of One who we know has the heart of a Father. – Dietrich Bonhoeffer

Praise is the first weapon in powerful prayer. Each of Jesus' recorded prayers starts with praise and we should copy Him. Luke 10:21 says:

> At that very time He rejoiced greatly in the Holy Spirit, and said, "I praise You, O Father, Lord of heaven and earth, that You have hidden these things from the wise and intelligent and have revealed them to infants. Yes, Father, for this way was well-pleasing in Your sight." (NASB)

It makes sense for praise to be the first part of prayer. When we begin to pray, we are ushered into the throne room of Almighty God – with the angels and seraphim. Other believers join us before God's throne. Throughout the Bible, the first response people make in God's presence is worship.

Why is praise a powerful weapon when we pray?

We were created to love God and people, but because of original sin, we found ourselves in circumstances where we hurt others, and others hurt us. Soon we developed the idea our main task was to guard our heart. We built walls to keep others out. Occasionally, we would let someone in, but doing so terrified us, and we soon found a reason to kick them out.

The result is we have small hearts. In fact, as time passed our hearts grew smaller and smaller.

Praise is an important weapon in the war room of prayer because it makes our hearts bigger – we understand who God is and what He can do

Praise opens our heart to God. Praise connects us with the Everlasting Father. Praise pulls us out of our little world and gives us the bigger picture of God's sovereign kingdom.

When I start my prayer with praise, it sounds something like this:

> *Heavenly Father. I praise you. You are good. You are strong. You are our deliverer. You are the Everlasting One. You set a table before us. You lead us to green pastors. There is none like you. Awesome in all your deeds. Your hand is not too short to save. You have loved us with an everlasting love.*

This is an example of a prayer of praise. Practice praising God in prayer until you feel your heart is bigger and you see God in His splendor. I use this hand motion to remind myself which part of prayer I am doing.

After you spend time praising God, move to the next weapon of powerful prayer: repentance.

Repent

If you find your life of prayer to be always so short, and so easy, and so spiritual, as to be without cost and strain and sweat to you, you may depend upon it, you have not yet begun to pray.
– Alexander Whyte

The second weapon of powerful prayer is repentance. I've noticed when I praise God with all my heart, I become more aware of my sin. When I see holy God, I also see my faults.

Feelings of inadequacy, fears, struggles, and other difficulties rise from my heart. In fact, I question whether I am praising God with all of my heart if this doesn't happen!

How do you deal with those negative thoughts and feelings? Jesus shared a parable about two different ways people deal with their sin in Luke 18:9-14:

Jesus told a story to some people who thought they were better than others and who looked down on everyone else:
Two men went into the temple to pray. One was a Pharisee and the other a tax collector. The Pharisee stood over by himself and prayed, "God, I thank you that I am not greedy, dishonest, and unfaithful in marriage like other people. And I am really glad that I am not like that tax collector over there. I go without eating for two days a week, and I give you one tenth of all I earn."

The tax collector stood off at a distance and did not think he was good enough even to look up toward heaven. He was so sorry for what he had done that he pounded his chest and prayed, "God, have pity on me! I am such a sinner."

Then Jesus said, "When the two men went home, it was the tax

*collector and not the Pharisee who was pleasing to God. If you
put yourself above others, you will be put down. But if you
humble yourself, you will be honored." (CEV)*

Some people don't deal with their sin when they pray. Instead, they think about their good deeds and the bad deeds of others. Psychologists call this misdirection. The Pharisee in Jesus' parable hardened his heart by judging others. Throughout the Bible, God cautions He will not listen to a hard-hearted person.

People like the tax collector choose to repent of their sins – owning their faults. Repenting means to admit our sin openly, feel remorse, and turn away from committing it again. This is what the tax collector did, and Jesus said he went home justified – God had heard his prayer. Repenting pleases God and connects us with His heart when we pray.

People are uncomfortable with the idea we will all face a judgment day. We feel like we are barely keeping up with our lives as it is and rationalize that God will overlook our sin. We spurn judgment day because our hearts are stubborn. We don't want to admit our wrongdoing and come up with flimsy excuses to explain it away. Comparing ourselves with others is how we usually do this. We say, "I'm not like ISIS, or people who riot, or…"

When God brings up the truth of my sin, I have two choices: I can repent or I can harden my heart. Repentance is a powerful prayer weapon in the war room, because our hearts are hard and need to be soft towards God.

When I pray the "repent" part of my prayers, I talk to God saying:

*Lord, forgive me for my anger and how I treated my friend yes-
terday. I was thinking selfishly and pushing my agenda. I hurt
her, and I am sorry. I could tell you were displeased and you
have convicted me several times since then, but I haven't cared
and have hardened my heart. Please forgive me and help me as I
apologize to my friend today. Soften my heart towards you and
her. I repent of my sin.*

Your prayer will be different, but I wanted to provide an
example. Here is the "repent" hand motion.

After spending time repenting of your sins and softening your
heart before God, move to the third weapon of powerful
prayer: asking.

To download *Powerful Prayers in the War Room* on Amazon
CLICK HERE.

BOOKS BY THE AUTHOR

Battle Plan for Prayer Series

Powerful Prayers in the War Room equips you to become a powerful prayer warrior and bring healing and hope to your family and friends. Perfect for small group Bible study.

Powerful Worship in the War Room teaches groups of believers – family or friends – a powerful and practical way to obey the Great Commandment together.

Powerful Jesus in the War Room will strengthen your prayer life by showing you how to connect your personality to one of the eight love languages of Jesus.

Powerful Promises in the War Room is a collection of 100 promises to hide in your heart and defeat Satan in spiritual warfare.

Follow Jesus Training Series

Making Radical Disciples: How to Make Disciples who Multiply Disciples Using Ten Easy-To-Teach Christ-Centered Discipleship Lessons.

Training Radical Leaders: How to Equip Leaders who Develop Leaders Using Ten Christ-Centered Leadership Bible Studies

Starting Radical Churches: How to Start A House Church that Starts New House Churches Using Ten Christ-Centered Church Planting Bible Studies.

Christian Self-Help Guides

Fear is a Liar: How to Stop Anxious Thoughts and Feel God's Love Again. Perfect for Small Group Bible Study.

Shame is a Liar: How to Find Inner Healing and Strength Every Day *(March 2020)*

ABOUT THE AUTHOR

Daniel B Lancaster (PhD) enjoys training others to become passionate followers of Christ. He has planted two churches in America and trained over 5,000 people in Southeast Asia as a strategy coordinator with the *International Mission Board*. He served as Assistant Vice-President for University Ministries at *Union University* and currently is a international missionary with *Cornerstone International*. He has four grown children and a delightful grandson.

Dr. Dan is available for speaking and training events. Contact him at dan@lightkeeperbooks.com to arrange a meeting for your group. All his books are available on Amazon.com.

Made in the USA
Coppell, TX
02 December 2020